THE WRITINGS OF JOSEP LLUÍS SERT

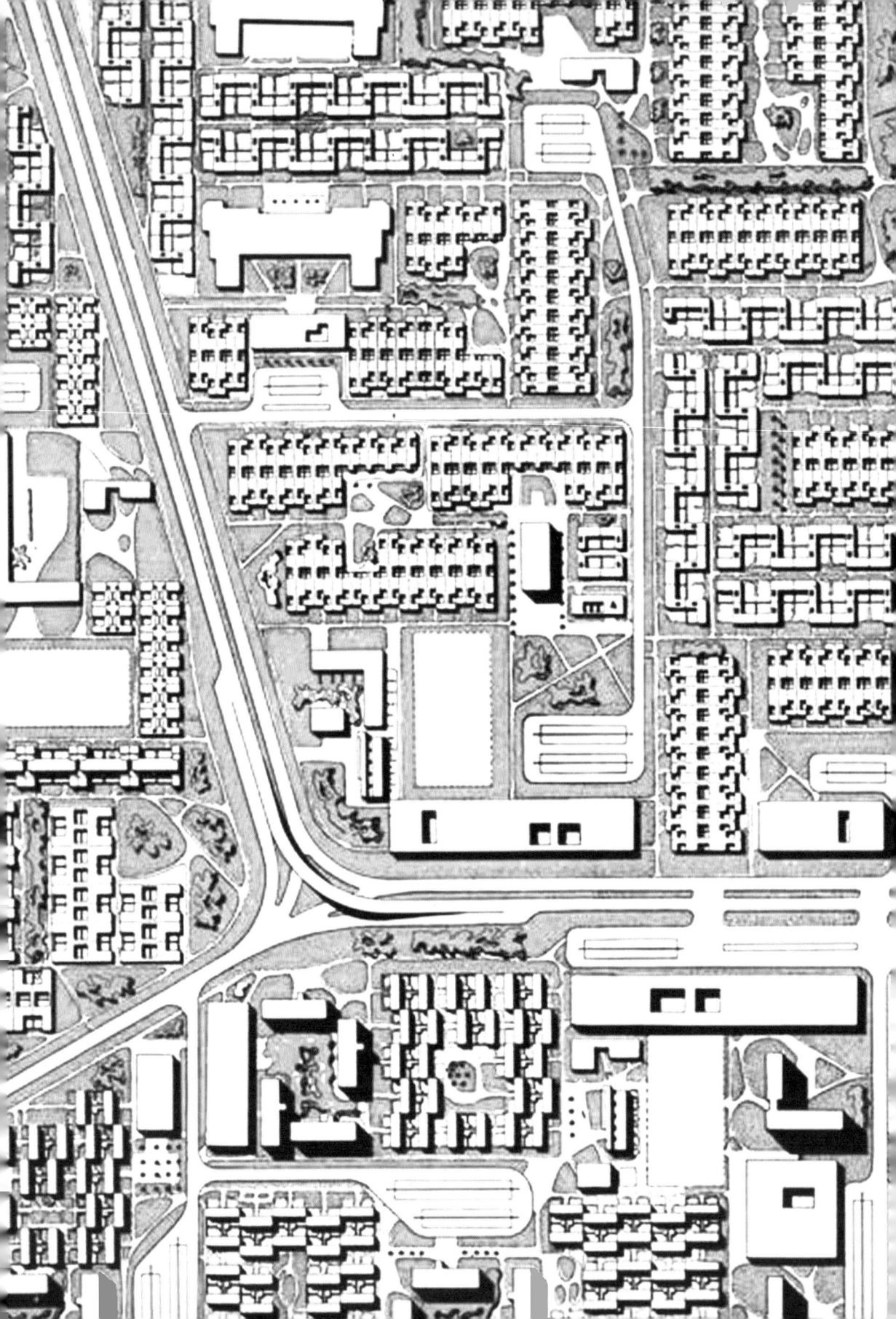

even
THE WRITINGS OF JOSEP LLUÍS SERT

EDITED BY **ERIC MUMFORD** FOREWORD BY **MOHSEN MOSTAFAVI**

Yale University Press New Haven and London **Harvard Graduate School of Design** Cambridge

Published with assistance from the Harvard Graduate School of Design Department of Publications.

Copyright © 2015 Harvard University Graduate School of Design (Sert essays) and Eric Mumford (introductions).

All rights reserved.

This book may not be reproduced, in whole or in part, including illustrations, in any form (beyond that copying permitted by Sections 107 and 108 of the U.S. Copyright Law and except by reviewers for the public press), without written permission from the publishers.

yalebooks.com/art

Designed by Jena Sher
Set in EideticNeo, Elena and Galaxie Polaris type by Jena Sher
Printed in China by Regent Publishing Services Limited

Library of Congress Control Number: 2014939883
ISBN 978-0-300-20739-2

A catalogue record for this book is available from the British Library.
This paper meets the requirements of ANSI/NISO Z 39.48-1992 (Permanence of Paper).

10 9 8 7 6 5 4 3 2 1

Frontispiece: Town Planning Associates, Chimbote Masterplan, 1948 (detail; see page 18).
p. vi: Sert, Jackson & Associates, Peabody Terrace Married Student Housing, 1963 (detail; see p. 120).
Cover illustration: Josep Lluís Sert, sketch from India, 1970 (detail; see p. 127).

CONTENTS

VI	**FOREWORD** by Mohsen Mostafavi
XII	**INTRODUCTION** by Eric Mumford
1	**1** THE THEME OF THE CONGRESS THE CORE
11	**2** THE NEIGHBORHOOD UNIT A HUMAN MEASURE IN CITY PLANNING
33	**3** URBAN DESIGN
41	**4** ARCHITECTURE AND THE VISUAL ARTS
47	**5** NEW YORK ARCHITECTURE AND THE CITY
57	**6** CIAM X DUBROVNIK
69	**7** HARVARD URBAN PROBLEM AND OPPORTUNITY
79	**8** THE HUMAN SCALE KEY TO THE MEASURE OF CITIES
91	**9** ARCHITECTURAL FASHIONS AND THE PEOPLE
99	**10** BOSTON A LIVELY AND HUMAN CITY
107	**11** THE ROLE OF GOVERNMENT IN THE FORM AND ANIMATION OF THE URBAN CORE
111	**12** OPEN SPACES AND PEDESTRIAN PATHS IN THE UNIVERSITY
121	**13** SIGFRIED GIEDION IN MEMORIAM
125	**14** ARCHITECTURE AND THE PEOPLE THERE ARE TWO HISTORIES OF ARCHITECTURE
133	**15** INDUSTRIALIZATION AN OPPORTUNITY FOR THE DESIGN OF NEW COMMUNITIES
143	**16** BALANCE IN THE HUMAN HABITAT
154	ACKNOWLEDGMENTS
156	NOTES
159	TEXT SOURCES
160	INDEX
166	ILLUSTRATION CREDITS

FOREWORD
MOHSEN MOSTAFAVI

Few architects ever get the opportunity to radically transform the nature of practice. And that's probably how it should be, given that continuity and evolution, rather than reinvention, are the hallmarks of architecture. Unlike art, where freedom of realization is constrained only by the medium chosen (whether painting, sculpture, video, or installation), architecture and its allied design fields are systematically shaped by contingent conditions: those of client, site, program, materials, and budget. Buildings are complicated artifacts that invariably take a long time to realize. And architecture is a slow profession—a profession unaccustomed to change.

Every so often, however, someone exceptional comes along and helps to alter our conception of architecture and its practices. Ludwig Mies van der Rohe is one such person. Another is Le Corbusier, whose highly effective and sustained global impact can be attributed not just to the achievements of his projects and publications, or to the influence of CIAM (International Congresses for Modern Architecture), but also—and perhaps above all—to the organization and diverse geographical composition of his office. Le Corbusier's collaborators came to Paris from all over Europe and from India, Latin America, and Japan. Many of them took their experience of working in the office to new locations. They made his architecture somehow site-specific, and in the process made it their own.

A third transformative figure is Josep Lluís Sert (1902-1983). The long connection between Le Corbusier and Sert, a Spanish member of CIAM, is reflected in Sert's writings and projects. He championed, and subsequently supervised, Le Corbusier's only commission in the United States, the Carpenter Center for the Visual Arts at Harvard University—a project that Le Corbusier himself had little direct involvement with in the early 1960s. Despite this friendship and professional homage, Sert remained in many respects a Mediterranean architect. The culture of his native Barcelona was ingrained in his soul, informing even the projects he designed long after he had moved to the colder climate of Cambridge, Massachusetts.

Like many of his contemporaries, Sert built a number of residential projects, single-family homes for private clients, but his architecture is essentially urban in character. For him there is an inseparable bond between architecture and its public, and his projects are invariably imbued with a focus on social interaction.

At the Center for the Study of World Religions, his first project at Harvard, Sert used the concept of open-access galleries to link what are essentially studio rooms. At Holyoke Center he transplanted the idea of the galleria to the heart of Harvard Square. The disruption caused by wind and weather to the proper functioning of these buildings seems to have been secondary to the sense of urbanity he was seeking. Peabody Terrace, a large and primarily highrise graduate housing project in Cambridge, is another example of this attitude. Scale, color, window modulations, and orientation are all used to create a metropolitan feel for this architecturally significant project along the Charles River.

Alongside this incorporation of urban elements, there are other ways in which the reference to the urban is manifested in Sert's U.S. projects. One involves the idea of the city being in some sense ingested into the body of some of his larger buildings, such as the Science Center building at Harvard. The building's four entrances/exits help set up its capacity to act as an interior thoroughfare connecting the campus east-west and north-south, the experience of passage enlivened by the large cast relief by the sculptor Constantino Nivola on one of the long walls of the building.

In addition, the expansive ground floor is articulated as an interior plaza, a meeting place for large groups of students going in and out of the surrounding lecture halls, as if they were buildings on the edge of a public square. Harvard University's recent decision to create an exterior plaza adjacent to this building has reinforced the interconnections between the inside and the outside and brought a greater number of people to this location, emphasizing the urban dimension of Sert's architecture.

A further aspect of the interrelationship between architecture and the city in Sert's work is manifested through the concept of the urban fragment. In the postwar period many government agencies and academic institutions expanded the scale of their construction projects, buoyed by the optimism and confidence that came with the need to rebuild the economy and society. This middle or intermediary scale, between architecture and the city, is the domain of urban design.

Urban design provided the opportunity for these types of large civic projects to be considered as a whole or, as Sert put it, a "complete environment." Such an ambitious challenge required the bringing together of a diversity of design fields. To train professionals who could address these issues, Sert established the first urban design program at the Graduate School of Design in 1960. From its inception the program was seen as a way of integrating planning, architecture, and landscape architecture, and of operating in the space between them.

For Sert, urban design made it possible to reintroduce into city planning the measure related to human scale and social interaction. Historic cities or towns, he argued, were the physical manifestations of the "life of a community," but the rationalization of building for the service of capital had led to an increasingly homogeneous approach that undermined the distinctive identity of many areas. His report on the neighborhood unit offered a means to regain that sense of identity, presenting the cuadras of many Latin American cities, with their square blocks and big patios, as examples of the type of multifunctional public space that acts as a significant place of recreation and gathering for the community.

A key component of Sert's approach was to consider the various functions of the city in terms of their connections. His call for the integration of residential areas into cities is a warning against the dangers of isolated, monofunctional programs. For Sert, the neighborhood provides a specific logic of measure, of proximity of activities and relations, that is tied to the human body. But the concept of the neighborhood is also an argument for urban density, social values, and pedestrian networks, and a warning against the consequences of suburban sprawl.

Given Sert's repeated calls for an architecture of social relations, it is ironic that many of his larger buildings, though recognized for their programmatic innovations, have also been criticized for their aesthetic and material harshness. The choice of concrete as a building material, together with the relative mega-scale and programmatic diversity of Sert's institutional buildings, was bound up with his belief in the importance of a new type of urban architecture. The "toughness" of concrete, its "brutality," was seen to be necessary to produce a resilient form suited to metropolitan life.

Sert, Jackson & Gourley, Center for the Study of World Religions, Harvard University, 1959. View of interior courtyard galleries.

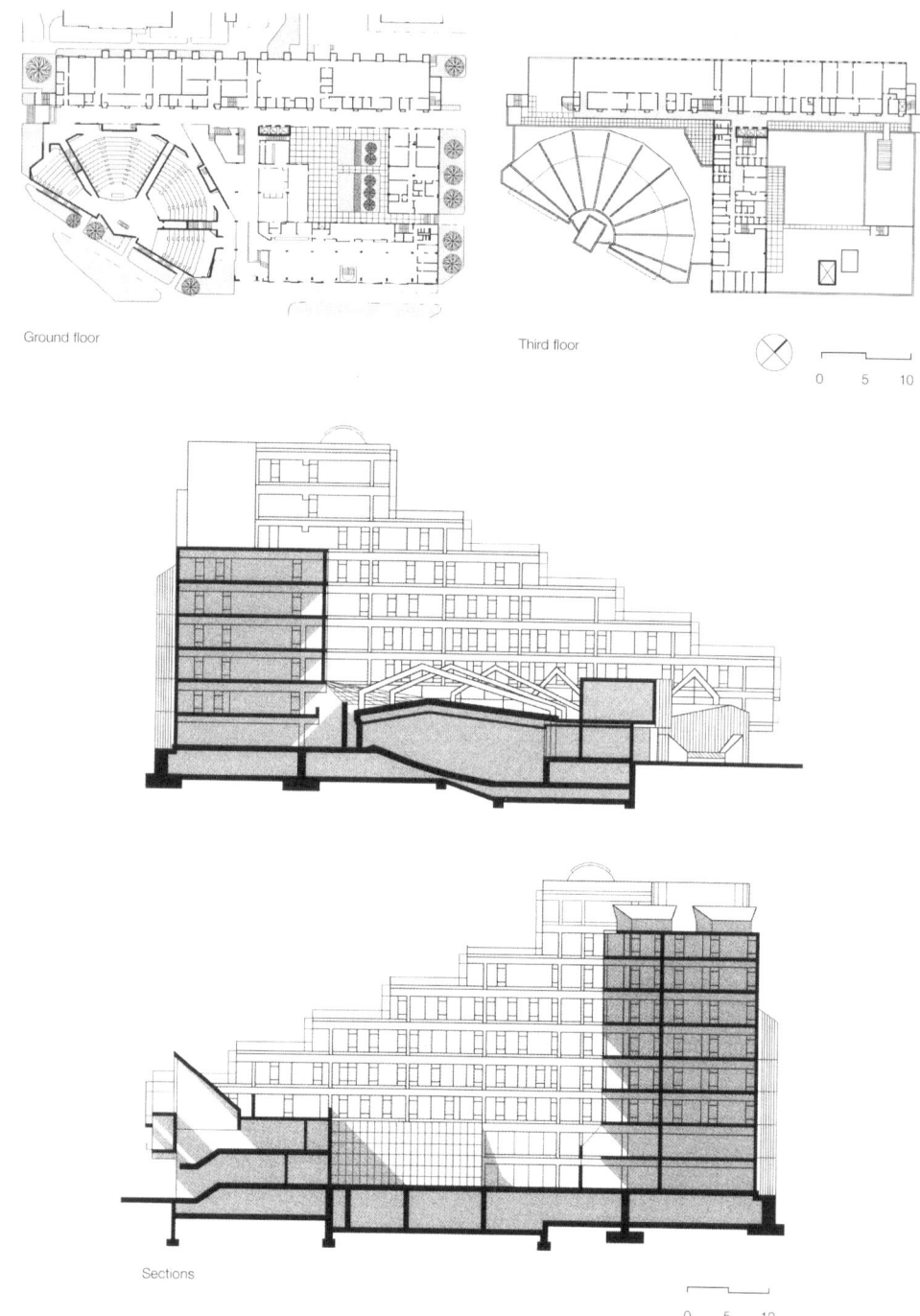

Sert, Jackson & Associates, Harvard University Science Center, 1968-73. Plans and sections.

Contantino Nivola, untitled plaster casting on sand, Harvard University Science Center, 1972. Originally installed in the BBPR Olivetti showroom, 584 Fifth Avenue, New York, 1953. The polychrome decoration was added in 1972.

While the freshness of the original materials and surfaces has diminished with age, the negative reaction to Sert's buildings is not simply based on their physical presence, but is a manifestation of our society's changing attitudes. The optimistic confidence of the postwar period, its willingness to embrace the new, has given way to an increasingly risk-averse sensibility.

The specific manner of appreciating and renovating Sert's architecture is particularly important as Harvard begins the important task of making architectural modifications to both the Science Center and Holyoke Center buildings; the latter will accommodate the university's new Smith Campus Center. How will the architects charged with this task respond to Sert's architecture? Will they attempt to "soften" it, to make it more appealing to a wider audience? Sert's architecture was designed with incredible bravura. At Harvard, the sheer scale and number of his projects represent the aspirations of an academic institution willing to lead and to take on the risks that this leadership entails.

The texts in this volume provide the background and the narrative structure to Sert's urban architecture. It is inspiring to see an architect take a position on such a diverse range of topics—and with a clarity akin to a manifesto. The reciprocities between these writings and his architecture are invariably in the service of the collective and the community. And the buildings, even though large and visible, are perhaps the closest a modern architect has come to producing what were historically thought of as "background" urban public buildings—their performative role as urban artifacts for the citizens overriding their claim to formal and aesthetic uniqueness.

But there is no one-to-one correlation between writing and building. One of the many values of Sert's essays lies in the impact of their critical rereading by the next generation of architects, planners, and landscape architects. In that sense, this book contains valuable seeds for renewed discussion about the future of our cities. There is much that we can learn from both the aspirations and the failures of the recent past as we imagine new ways of transforming our communities. Equally, Sert's writings provide the platform for reimagining the tasks of the practitioner and in turn the responsibilities of the academy as the place for the articulation of the pedagogy and discourse that will reshape practice.

Mohsen Mostafavi is dean, Harvard Graduate School of Design, and Alexander and Victoria Wiley Professor of Design.

INTRODUCTION
ERIC MUMFORD

Today the Barcelona-born architect Josep Lluís Sert (1902-1983) is remembered primarily for several reasons: his highly visible though sometimes still controversial work as an architect for Harvard and Boston Universities (1958-73) and for his mixed-income housing on Roosevelt Island in New York City (1970-75) and in Yonkers, New York (1970-73); his role as president of postwar CIAM (International Congresses for Modern Architecture) from 1947-56; and his position, from 1953-69, as dean of the Harvard Graduate School of Design, where he advocated and helped to found the profession of urban design. One could also add to all this his early involvement with the Spanish CIAM GATCPAC (Grup d'Arquitectes Catalans Per Una Arquitectura Contemporánea) group in Barcelona in the 1930s, before his immigration to the United States in 1939, and his subsequent, mostly unbuilt but widely published urban plans for Brazil, Peru, Colombia, Venezuela, and Cuba in the 1940s and 1950s.

Each of these aspects of his career has now been the subject of some scholarly work, but Sert remains a blurry and misunderstood figure in contemporary architectural culture.[1] As dean and Harvard campus architect, his work is still occasionally admired, but the linkages between this work and his various international activities—which included not only CIAM but also his involvement in United Nations' efforts on housing and urbanism from the 1950s to the 1970s—are often poorly understood and perhaps undervalued.

This may be because Sert himself never published much about his own work and ideas after his early collective CIAM publications, of which *Can Our Cities Survive?* (1942) and *CIAM 8: The*

Sert, Jackson & Associates, Roosevelt Island mixed-use housing for the New York State Urban Development Corporation, 1970-75. View of model.

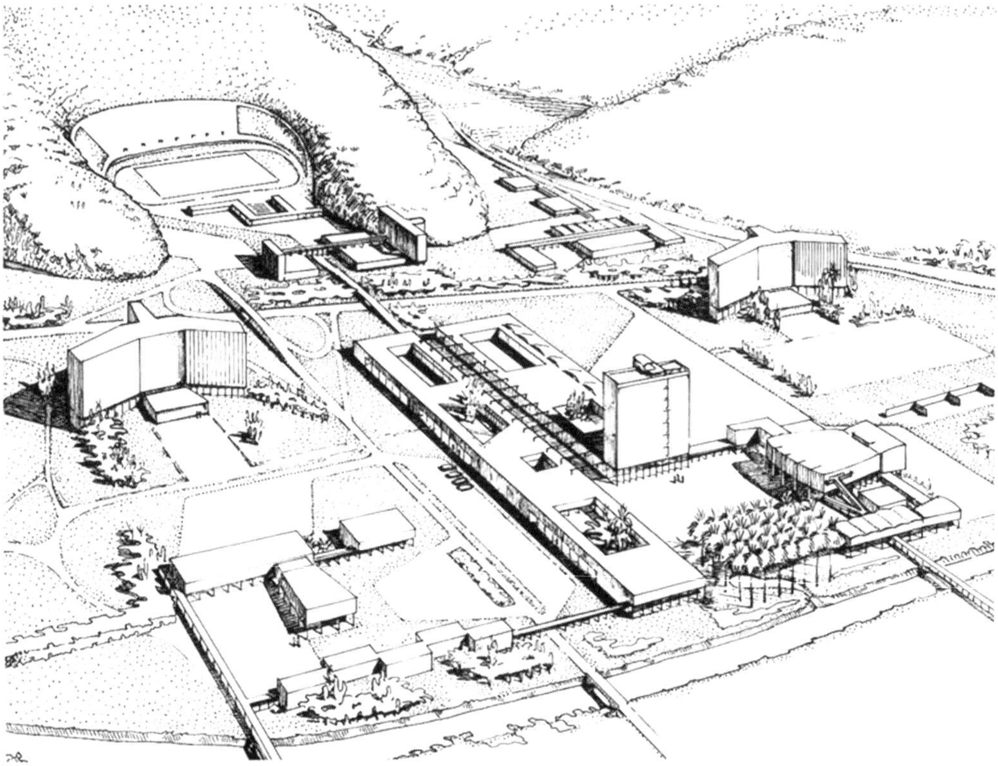

Town Planning Associates (Paul Lester Wiener, Josep Lluís Sert, and Paul Schulz), Brazilian Motor City, near Rio de Janeiro, 1944–47, third version of the project. Aerial perspective of the proposed pedestrian civic center.

Aerial view of La Candelaria (Old City), Bogotá, used by Sert in the first overview of his work. From Knud Bastlund, José Luis Sert: *Architecture, City Planning, Urban Design* (New York: Praeger, 1967), 66.

Heart of the City (1952) are the best known. *Can Our Cities Survive?* was the first English-language publication of CIAM concepts of the Functional City, and it embodies the major ideas of prewar CIAM. *The Heart of the City* indicated the shift from the mechanistic socialist utopias of prewar CIAM to pedestrian urbanism and the cultural and democratic importance of urban centrality for modern architects in the context of postwar urban decentralization. Sert never published the book that would have indicated the third phase in his urbanistic thinking, *Balanced Habitat,* related to his United Nations work in the 1970s and indicating his engagement with issues of urban sustainability, housing typologies, and mixed use in ways that can still seem relevant today.[2]

This book is an effort to make some of Sert's previously unpublished writings available to a wider audience. This may change the usual image of him to some degree, showing that he was not simply a Corbusian campus and housing architect and CIAM administrator. It demonstrates through his own writings his articulation of the reasons for the CIAM focus on the heart of the city and his wide-ranging efforts to advance various aspects of urban design. As Sert defined it, this field was an effort to develop a new profession where architecture, landscape architecture, and city and regional planning all overlapped.[3] These three previously separate professional fields had been linked by architecture dean Joseph Hudnut in 1936 to create the Harvard Graduate School of Design (GSD), which Hudnut saw "as parts of a common field having processes and objectives which are and should be in many respects identical." In line with CIAM, by 1940 Hudnut saw all three disciplines as "inseparable . . . from the collective life, the smallest unit of which is the family, the largest the population of a city or a region." Hudnut also emphasized that all three shared a concern for the "expressive values of three-dimensional forms," and he understood "design" at the GSD to mean "first, an arrangement of ideas, and, second, an arrangement of visible forms which interpret those ideas."[4]

Hudnut's effort to link these professional fields has remained central to the GSD, despite Hudnut's own falling out with Walter Gropius several years after Hudnut had hired him as chair of architecture there in 1937.[5] Taking over as dean on Gropius's recommendation in 1953 in the wake of the contentious resignations of both men, Sert continued the GSD focus on integrative three-dimensional design across these fields. But he also introduced the field of urban design as a linking element among them at the famous 1956 Harvard conference on the topic.[6] In doing so, Sert put an unprecedented emphasis on design at the pedestrian heart of the city, distancing the GSD from the Gropius-era focus on designing Greenbelt town-like suburban settlements near express highways.

As some of these texts demonstrate, Sert instead was a strong and early advocate of the importance of pedestrian cities to contemporary politics and culture. Although he looked to the work of Louis Kahn and Edmund Bacon in Philadelphia as a partial model for urban design, his own work also makes evident what he thought design professionals should do in response to the growing complexity and confusions of postwar urban development in an era dominated by automobiles and the increasing appeal of suburbia. From his many mostly unbuilt South American and Cuban urban projects to highly visible built work such as Peabody Terrace student housing at Harvard and the housing on Roosevelt Island and in Yonkers, New York, Sert proposed and was occasionally able to build urban interventions that created varied outdoor and indoor pedestrian circulation routes and urban plazas within complex mixed-use site organizations. These accommodated structured parking and urban landscaping, responding to specific urban and cultural contexts in ways that are still often not well understood, often because of the rejection of Corbusian modern architecture that began even as they were being completed.

The writings included here also help to counter persistent misunderstandings of Sert (and of the work and intentions of some of his CIAM colleagues) that have created a kind of intellectual void in how current approaches to urban design developed after 1956. In what had been, until recently, the widespread popular historical understanding of twentieth-century urban development, American cities were thought to have been vital pedestrian and mass-transit environments until misguided postwar modernist planners destroyed them with slum clearance, highways, and highrise housing like the Pruitt-Igoe complex in St. Louis. Recent scholarship has shown this model to be largely a New Urbanist myth, in that long-standing patterns of peripheral growth and a preference for automobiles over mass transit were evident in American cities as early as the 1920s. The advantages of centralized, pedestrian-oriented urban living were rarely valued until the late 1950s, at precisely the moment when these older urban patterns were beginning to disappear from many cities. It is in this context, one that also produced both the American interstate system and government funded efforts to "save" downtowns with urban renewal, that Sert began to advocate the advantages of pedestrian urbanism. It was also, of course, the point when issues of racial integration, alluded to by Charles Abrams at the first Harvard Urban Design Conference, began to reshape American life and politics.[7]

In the development of urban design as a professional field, Sert and parallel figures like his CIAM associate Ernesto Rogers in Italy, a partner in the Milan firm BBPR and a GSD visitor in 1954, had begun to substantially modify CIAM's prewar urbanism based on the "four functions" of dwelling, work, transportation, and recreation before the 1954 challenge of Team 10 to CIAM over this issue.[8] This may seem surprising, given Sert's central role in CIAM at this time, but it was Sert's postwar advocacy in CIAM of the importance of central pedestrian areas to progressive cultural and political life that helped define an entire generation of modernist urban preoccupations. These arguably had an effect on Team 10 and its successor groups' preoccupations as well.

This collection of mostly unpublished Sert writings from 1951 to 1977 makes this less well-known side of Sert's work accessible for the first time, and allows for a more balanced assessment of his historical importance to late twentieth-century urbanism. While there is no question that he was often assisted by Jaqueline Tyrwhitt (1905-1983) in his CIAM and Harvard Urban Design publications and activities, there is also no evidence that these texts were not Sert's own work. The level of finish varies from text to text—some are more or less rough lecture transcriptions, while others show evidence of considerable editing for style—but the basic ideas and means of expression remain remarkably similar over the thirty-year period during which they were written.

Perhaps also surprising to those who see Sert's urbanistic views as the same as those of prewar CIAM, Sert's unpublished writings here indicate how his urbanistic proposals differ from those of Le Corbusier, whom he nonetheless often cited as his main inspiration throughout his career.[9] They reveal that by the 1950s Sert had firmly rejected what he called the "functionalist dream cities of the 1920s" and that he instead admired the active pedestrian street life of cities like Bogotá, Medellín, New York, Boston, and San Francisco.[10] In his work with Le Corbusier around 1950 on planning for Bogotá, Sert and his partner Paul Lester Wiener produced their own version of the Bogotá masterplan, which differs significantly from Le Corbusier's proposals for total urban clearance and rebuilding with highrise slab housing blocks. Instead of calling for the clearance of the old city, the district of La Candelaria, Sert and Wiener proposed its retention, and in their concept plans for new neighborhood sectors they proposed a range of pedestrian-oriented residential types and communal buildings that were more adapted to local culture than was Le Corbusier's more familiar Unité model.[11] Yet Sert, like his CIAM colleagues, was by no means primarily an urban preservationist, and like other modern architects he saw the salvation of the pedestrian city to be in its modernist rebuilding, a position controversially quite evident in their proposed interventions for the old city in his and Wiener's Havana Plan of 1955-58.[12] By 1961, related but more radical ideas about the importance of street life would soon be developed by Jane Jacobs (who had commented at the First Harvard Urban Design Conference) into a full-fledged rejection of urban renewal and modernism. Jacobs's total rejection of master planning was a step that Sert himself was never willing to take.[13]

In 1960, Sert also launched the world's first professional master of urban design program at Harvard. This was a joint degree program in which all the students were also professional master's degree students in architecture, landscape architecture, or planning. To head this program, he hired Willo von Moltke in 1961, a planning associate of Edmund N. Bacon in Philadelphia in 1954-61. Von Moltke (1911-1987) had overseen the urban design plan for the Society Hill area and the housing work of I. M. Pei there, and was appointed tenured director of the Harvard program in 1964, a position he retained until 1977. Various other eminent faculty taught in Sert's Urban Design program, including Tyrwhitt, the landscape architect Hideo Sasaki, the architectural historian Eduard Sekler, and Jerzy Soltan, the Polish Corbusian associate and peripheral Team 10 member who was also chair of architecture at GSD from 1967 to 1975. The GSD urban design program also included Tokyo architect Fumihiko Maki (1962-65) and various visitors, such as the Team 10 member Shadrach Woods. Sert also introduced the use of computers into urban design at the GSD at this time and chose the architect of its new building, John Andrews, before his retirement there as dean in 1969.

By then the modernist planning direction that Sert represented—however much modified in his version as pedestrian-oriented urban design—was under challenge from a variety of directions, and his efforts at GSD are still sometimes criticized. And in fact at this time he did want to tear down Harvard's Memorial Hall and was indeed in close contact with advocates of urban renewal like Charles Abrams and government officials like Robert C. Weaver, the first African-American cabinet member and first secretary of Housing and Urban Development (HUD), who in a paternalistic, design-driven way were attempting to remake American metropolitan areas in what they thought were progressive directions. In the United States, of course, most of these efforts, which involved much displacement and demolition, became the focus of intense conflict and resentment during that era of Civil Rights and Vietnam War protests.

Among Sert's last major works were two large projects commissioned by the New York State Urban Development Corporation (UDC) in 1970 for housing at the "new town in-town" of Roosevelt Island, and one in Yonkers, New York. These works attempted to modify typical American public housing patterns by including more communal facilities within them. At about the same time Sert became active in efforts to promote the United Nations' focus on Human Settlements, which resulted in the Habitat II conference in Vancouver in 1976, where he advocated similar models for housing worldwide.

By this point Sert's focus was on the dangers to both the urban quality of life and the broader natural environment, and which he planned to offer some design solutions for in an unfinished book, *Balanced Habitat* (1977). He also continued to practice architecture in Boston and near his summer residence in Ibiza, Spain, until his death in 1983. In subsequent years much of his built work, and certainly his unbuilt Latin American urban plans, were not seen as very important to the field. Because they were commissioned by a variety of postwar governments, some quite authoritarian, under complicated circumstances that tied them to Cold War American foreign policy, the innovative nature of the design ideas contained in them is often overlooked. Many urban design ideas that Sert sought to turn into a set of principles, such as the use of the dense fabric of courtyard houses, the abstracted use of the organizational patterns of historical buildings and spaces, a sensitivity to existing urban contexts, and the use of systems of urban greenways and pedestrian paths are perhaps now better known in association with other figures within the same CIAM and post-CIAM orbit—such as Le Corbusier, Maxwell Fry & Jane Drew, and Pierre Jeanneret at Chandigarh, or the housing concepts of Serge Chermayeff, Fumihiko Maki, and some members of Team 10. Yet all of these ideas are present in Sert's mostly unbuilt plans from 1947 forward.

Until recently there has also been little awareness of how Sert's urbanistic ideas differed from Le Corbusier's, and of his important role in advancing his ideas in the context of trying to create "balanced habitat." This collection of writings is intended to change this perception, and to make clear Sert's importance as an early and talented advocate of ideas about the importance of pedestrian urbanism and of cities designed in relation to the natural environment that have in many cases become a part of mainstream design culture.

1
THE THEME OF THE CONGRESS
THE CORE (1951)

This is the transcript from the CIAM Archives at the ETH Zurich of Sert's opening remarks at CIAM 8, the "Heart of the City" Congress, held in Hoddesdon, near London, in July 1951. It differs considerably from the published version of Sert's remarks in the conference publication assembled by Jaqueline Tyrwhitt as *CIAM 8: The Heart of the City* (New York: Pellegrini and Cudahy, 1952) and has never been previously published.[1]
EM

The MARS group suggested "the core" as the theme for our Congress. We thought from the first that this was a very interesting subject, but in studying it, we found it rather difficult because it has not been explored before: but precisely because it has not been explored, it becomes a CIAM subject; CIAM has always pioneered this kind of work.

We do not pretend in this Congress to exhaust this subject, to explain it completely and to come to final conclusions, but we can make a start on a new study which can be extremely interesting, and that is what we would like to do.

Now at this point, I would like to stress that in the last years we have been studying many subjects that have to do with city planning. We have even made some studios on regional planning and on studies of a city as a whole. These studies affected communications, residential areas, industrial areas, zoning, and land use in general; but we always got to a point that we shunned and found very difficult. This was the center, the heart of the city or the core of the city, whichever you may like to call it.

There is no doubt that civic planning in the last few years has been escaping to the suburbs; urbanism has really become suburbanism. The majority of treatises that we see on city planning deal much more with suburban development, of the garden city type of development, and with other problems that have nothing to do with the core or the heart of the city. This has corresponded to the trend of decentralization in cities. The majority of people in the cities have gone suburban. Town planners have also become suburban and have followed this trend, but now we find that if we want to do something with our cities we have again to talk in civic and urban terms, and we believe we must tackle the difficult problem of the core of the city.

It is constantly said in popular magazines, and you hear it all around, that in the suburbs the way of living can be a paradise, with one's own radio and one's own television screen, a garden and an orchard, [with one] only needing to go to the city to work. The city is a disagreeable place where you only go to work, and which you leave as soon as you can by the fastest means of transportation along the best parkways, etc.

As city planners, and following the more humanistic approach to the city that CIAM has always taken, we should be against this stand. If life in a city is to be that kind of life, it is not worthwhile living in the city at all. We can possibly then consider that the dispersion or the decentralization should be total, and the city should disappear.

There is only one real advantage of living in a city, and that is to get man together with man, and to get people to exchange ideas and be able to discuss them freely. If one lives the kind of life that is dependent on good means of transportation to the suburbs and upon whatever

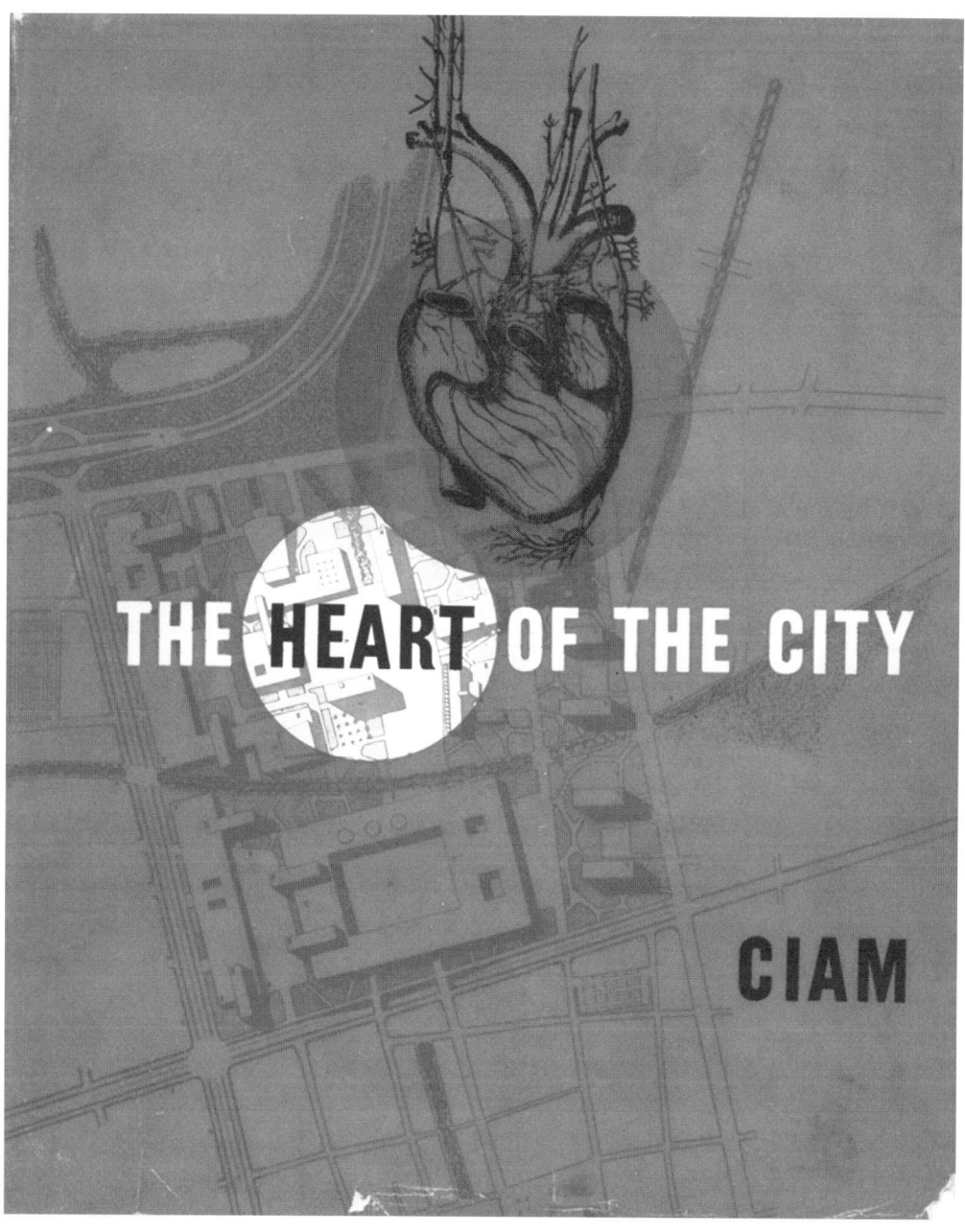

Dust jacket of J. Tyrwhitt, J. L. Sert, and E. N. Rogers, *CIAM 8: The Heart of the City* (New York: Pellegrini and Cudahy, 1952) showing a Town Planning Associates project for Cali, Colombia, with a mixed-use urban core that included a multistory commercial center.

Sert, sketch of Carnival parade in Rio de Janeiro, 1946.

news or information or vision or images can come through on a television frame or a radio loudspeaker, one no longer has initiative; one sees what one is shown and hears what one is told. That may be a terribly dangerous affair if the people who direct the speeches or the news, or show you the views on the television screen, do it according to their own views, which may be the wrong views. Then the people in the suburbs would see and hear only what those other people want them to see and hear. That would interfere very directly with our choice, and our freedom, of selecting one thing from another. Besides, the more the people are kept apart, the less they can exchange ideas and the more they are influenced by what they see or what they are given.

The city has become a terribly overextended monstrosity. The means of communication and contact and connection are so difficult that the people, because of the physical difficulties, get together less. This dispersion is dangerous and it can result in the destruction of the city, not only the destruction of the spiritual values of the city, but also the destruction of the city as an economic unit. It has been shown by figures today that the overextended cities and the overextended suburbs bring about bankruptcy of the municipal finances for reasons or factors that you know about.

So what we are going to try to do with this study of the core of the city is to see how, by means of establishing a system of cores, we can work out the reverse process of what has been called decentralization; a process we can call recentralization, to build up units and communities around centers that would bring them together.

If we have no centers to bring the communities together, the dispersion will continue. It can continue indefinitely. It is continuing without any limits. What we would like is to get a core or a nucleus reestablished—a thing which all the cities had before but which has been destroyed in our cities today. Now, of course, we are perfectly aware that this core cannot be reestablished just as it was in the old cities. It will be a core that corresponds to a new type of life and a new type of city. The old cores corresponded to the type of life of the old cities.

Aerial view of Cuzco, Peru, 1951. From Paul Lester Wiener and José Luis Sert, *Urbanisme en Amerique du Sud/Town-Planning in South America* (Paris: L'architecture d'aujourd'hui, 1951), 36.

At a certain moment in the history of civic development, these cores melted down, then disappeared. They have now been broken to pieces with the extension and overextension of the suburbs, so that today if there are some survivals of these cores, they do not really work, and are not as important, as in the cities of the past.

I believe new cores are necessary in our life today, because I believe people should be able to get together to exchange ideas and to discuss, to shake hands and look at each other directly and talk on all the things that are extremely important for our way of living if we are to keep a civic life which we believe in. We all agree that there has to be planned use of the land; parts of the land have to be allocated for residential purposes, parts for commerce, business, industry, recreations, etc. So when we subdivide the land and establish a land-use plan, we should establish for each of the different sectors a core or nucleus that would constitute the center or subcenter of those sectors.

Now these centers as announced in the program presented by MARS can, of course, correspond to units of different scales. They can exist in a practical form in a small-scale residential unit in a small town or village of a large size; in a neighborhood unit; in a residential district or a sector of the city as we call it. They add up to the center of the fairly large city and to the center of the metropolis (or a cluster of cities). So you will find that from the smallest to the biggest, there is a series of cores or nuclei that have definite functions. The basic function is always that of getting the people of a sector of the community together, and to establish some kind of community life that is focused or concentrated on that point, or at that core. The effect of this would be to establish a series of units whose centers would form a network of cores throughout the community. This could form—has been said by one of our friends who gave a talk recently in the United States—a constellation of communities or a constellation of units, the whole tied together and related by the different cores.

In talking about the possible dangers of the new means of telecommunication in breaking up the city, we should also recognize that these new means of communication can be enormously important in building up new cores.

You see today in the remotest cities in South America, or in any other continent in rapid development, how important it is for people to have, in the public square or in the place where they meet, a loudspeaker that gives them the latest news. Newspapers, which used to take days or weeks to arrive, can reach these cities today a few hours after they are published in the capital. Also very soon they will have television screens showing the possibilities of visual education in these places.

These means, if properly used, are of enormous importance in the core, especially in the small cores. They can put these people in immediate contact with the world. All the small public squares in the villages could really be like balconies to the outside world. The people would come there; the poorest people, who have no radio, could listen to the loudspeaker on the public square. They could see the images on the television screen. They could hear the news and have the paper from the next country in a few hours. That means that the small core can become more important if it benefits by this new means of communication and is not dissolved because of this new means of communication.

We have not heard many people talk for this new organization of the cities based on the core; but amid the mobility of today, one cannot find any more important element to bring

Sert, residence at Lattingtown Harbor Estates, Locust Valley, New York, 1949. Interior view, with Medellín masterplan on the wall to the left.

people together than the good development planning and construction of these cores. I do not see ... how we can form new cities or redevelop the old cities if we do not start with the place where the people have to meet, where the people have to exchange ideas, where the people can know what planning and other things mean to them.

We started in CIAM by doing other things that are very necessary—new residential units, slum clearance, etc.—but now when you go around the world, you find that in many countries it is much more important to give the people a small core where they could have the necessary educational means at hand, where they could see and hear about what the outside world is like, where they could have perhaps [basic] medical services, etc., shopping for the most essential articles: places where they can get some visual education by being shown pictures of any kind. That is much more important for what we want to carry out than other work that we are trying to do. I think that by getting at the core, by trying to re-plan the core, we would accelerate this process considerably. That is why we believe that this question of the core is terribly important and why we believe that CIAM should study it. It has been said that it would be very good, very useful, to have the help of other people—sociologists, mainly—who could help us with this problem. We all agree it would be convenient, but it is very difficult to find the right people to work with, and perhaps ... we [should] start this adventure on our own, ourselves, and then get outside help when we need it. We can invite criticism of our program. We do not pretend to do anything final or perfect, so we are open to all criticism, and we are very open to any suggestions that can come from outside, from people of other specializations.

The role of the architect in the core is a special one. We agree that cores should be planned, like all important city planning work, by a team of specialists, and that we should get outside help from other people specialized in other subjects; but we believe that the architect and planner have a very important role in planning this core and we also believe that there are some general principles on which the architect is perfectly clear.

Let us start with the simplest of ideas. We all live in big cities or know them. We all know how difficult it is to circulate in the center of the city, and we all know how traffic and mechanized means of transportation have taken over the center of the city and run, crisscrossed wildly, in all directions, and that the pedestrian really hasn't got a place to meet or rest or to feel like a citizen in a place of his own. There is already a recognized trend—as you will see from the plans displayed—that certain sectors in the center of cities should be left for pedestrians; where, if there is traffic, it is limited to certain hours, and the rest of the traffic remains outside this area.

This is a thing that has general application. From the biggest to the smallest, the core should always be an island for the pedestrian, where he feels safe, where he feels happy, where he can rest and be at ease. That means that this island should be fed by means of communication coming from everywhere but remaining outside the core. The parking area should be more or less screened on the outside. There are other points that the plans have in common, and it is encouraging to see how in spite of the distance and not exchanging thoughts on many of these ideas, different groups in different countries have come practically to the same conclusions.

It is difficult to establish a program for the core because each program will depend on many things. I know it would be much more satisfactory for many people to get a set of standards and say, "This is the way we have to do it." But like other problems in city planning, it is very difficult to establish those standards. First of all, there is the problem of scale. The cores must be completely different. It is clear that in a small neighborhood the needs are different, and the means are different from a big city center. In between are all the intermediate stages. Also there are differences because countries are different. The problems of climate create terrific differences, also the problems of standards of living, means, customs, and many other factors. So to try to give programs or general standards for cores would be a very difficult task. But I think that the work of the Congress may help in defining these matters and perhaps in giving broad programs for some of the more basic types.

I think the definition of the core, as given by the MARS group in their program, is a very good one and should be kept in mind during our work here. They say in their program that a community is not merely an aggregate of individuals, and that an essential feature in any true organism (such as the community) is a physical heart or nucleus, which we call the core. They go on to say that a community of people is a self-conscious organism, and that the members not only are dependent on one another, but each of them knows he is so dependent. This awareness or sense of community is expressed with varying degrees of intensity at different scale levels. It is very strong, for example, at the lowest scale levels, that of the family, emerges again strongly at five different levels above this, in the village or primary housing group, in the small market center or residential neighborhood, in the town or city center, in the city itself, and in the metropolis or multiple city. At each level, the creation of a special physical environment is called for, both as a setting for the expression of this sense of community and an actual expression of it. This is the physical heart of the community, the nucleus, the core.

I found rather a good statement on the core in a book by José Ortega y Gasset called *The Revolt of the Masses.* No doubt some of you are familiar with it. He says, "For in truth, the most accurate definition of the 'urbs' and the 'polis' is very like the comic definition of the cannon. You take a hole and wrap some steel wire tightly around it and that is your cannon. So the 'urbs' or the 'polis' starts at by being an empty space, the forum, the 'agora,' and all the rest is just a means of fixing that empty space, of limiting its outlines. The 'polis' is not primarily a collection of habitable dwellings, but a meeting place for citizens, a space set apart for public functions. The city is not built, as is the cottage or the 'domus,' to shelter from the weather and to propagate the species—these are personal, family concerns—but in order to discuss public affairs. Observe that this signifies nothing less than the invention of a new kind of space, much more now than the space of Einstein. Until then only one space existed, that of the open country, with all the consequences that this involves for the existence of man. The man of the fields is still a sort of vegetable. His existence, all that he feels, thinks, wishes for, preserves the listless drowsiness in which the plan lives. The great civilizations of Asia and Africa were, from this point of view, huge anthropomorphic vegetations. But the Greco-Roman decides to separate himself from the fields, from Nature, from the geo-botanic cosmos. How is this possible? How can man withdraw himself from the fields? Where will he go, since the earth is one huge unbounded field? Quite simple: he will mark off a portion of this field by means of walls which set up an enclosed finite space over against amorphous, limitless space. Here you have the public square. It is not, like the house, an 'interior' shut in from above, as are the caves which exist in the fields. It is purely and simply the negation of the fields. The square, thanks to the walls which enclose it, is a portion of the countryside which turns its back on the rest, eliminates the rest and sets up in opposition to it. This lesser rebellious field, which secedes from the limitless one, and keeps to itself, is a space *sui generis* of the most novel kind, in which man frees himself from the community of the plant and the animal, leaves them outside and creates a part which is purely human—a civil space."

This is important as it defines a civil space, or civic space, and I think that after our studies of bringing open space into the cities, we nonetheless feel the need for a civic space somewhere in them, and the most characteristic civic space will be precisely the core.

2
THE NEIGHBORHOOD UNIT
A HUMAN MEASURE IN CITY PLANNING (circa 1953)

This unpublished report was probably commissioned by Sert's CIAM colleague and former architectural partner Ernest Weissmann, the Zagreb-born architect who was the chief of the United Nations Housing and Town and Country Planning section in the Department of Social Affairs from 1951–55. Weissmann had worked with Le Corbusier at the same time as Sert in 1929, and the two émigrés designed an unbuilt New York City apartment house project in 1939. Weissmann then became an Allied wartime consultant on postwar reconstruction in Yugoslavia and a staff consultant to the United States Board of Economic Warfare from 1942–44, before becoming director of the industrial rehabilitation division of UNRRA, the United Nations Relief and Rehabilitation Administration, in Washington from 1944–47. He then held a variety of other U.N. posts until his retirement in 1974.

This text is an effort by Sert to explain the principles behind the urban design concepts he and Paul Lester Wiener had begun to propose in their Latin American planning work. These grew out of prewar American and English ideas about the "neighborhood unit," a term first used, as Sert notes here, by Clarence Perry in volume seven of The Regional Plan of New York and Environs in 1929, and then applied in CIAM by Maxwell Fry, Arthur Korn, and Felix Samuely in their MARS Plan of London, 1938–41. This design direction called for new residential areas to be designed in walkable patterns centered on elementary schools, as at Stein and Wright's Radburn, New Jersey (1928), where vehicular traffic was sorted by speed and kept away from pedestrian-accessible interior green areas.

Here Sert is critical of the many postwar housing projects that were not planned using such ideas. He also suggests that the "least developed countries" have not sufficiently considered whether Western models were applicable to their local conditions, anticipating Georges Candilis and Shadrach Woods (and subsequently Team 10) in arguing for modifying modernist planning models in relation to local cultures, climates, and building practices.[1] Sert also calls here for more flexible planning formulas that can change over time—"the task of the planner is not to try to adapt life to his plans, but [to] design his plans to fit the changing patterns of living." This essay also reiterates Sert's insistence that cities were already spatially overextended by 1953 and that "we should not carry this outward movement any further wherever possible."

EM

A village, a town, or a city is the physical expression of the life of a community; it is built or shaped to contain that community, to protect it, to shelter it and to hold it together as a social structure. In the past, neighborhoods within a city had a personality of their own. But as a rule, in late years they have become indistinguishable parts of the monotonous whole. They are cut up into blocks by streets congested with traffic, and they can no longer work and develop as a unit.

The city block as we know it today is only a group of buildings on plots of land which have been designed so that they can produce the greatest possible income. No land for community use is reserved and the acreage that is not sold goes to sidewalks and streets. These streets are not designed as meeting places or promenades, but only as elements of inter-communication connecting factory, shop or office to the home, that has its front door or garden gate right on the street.

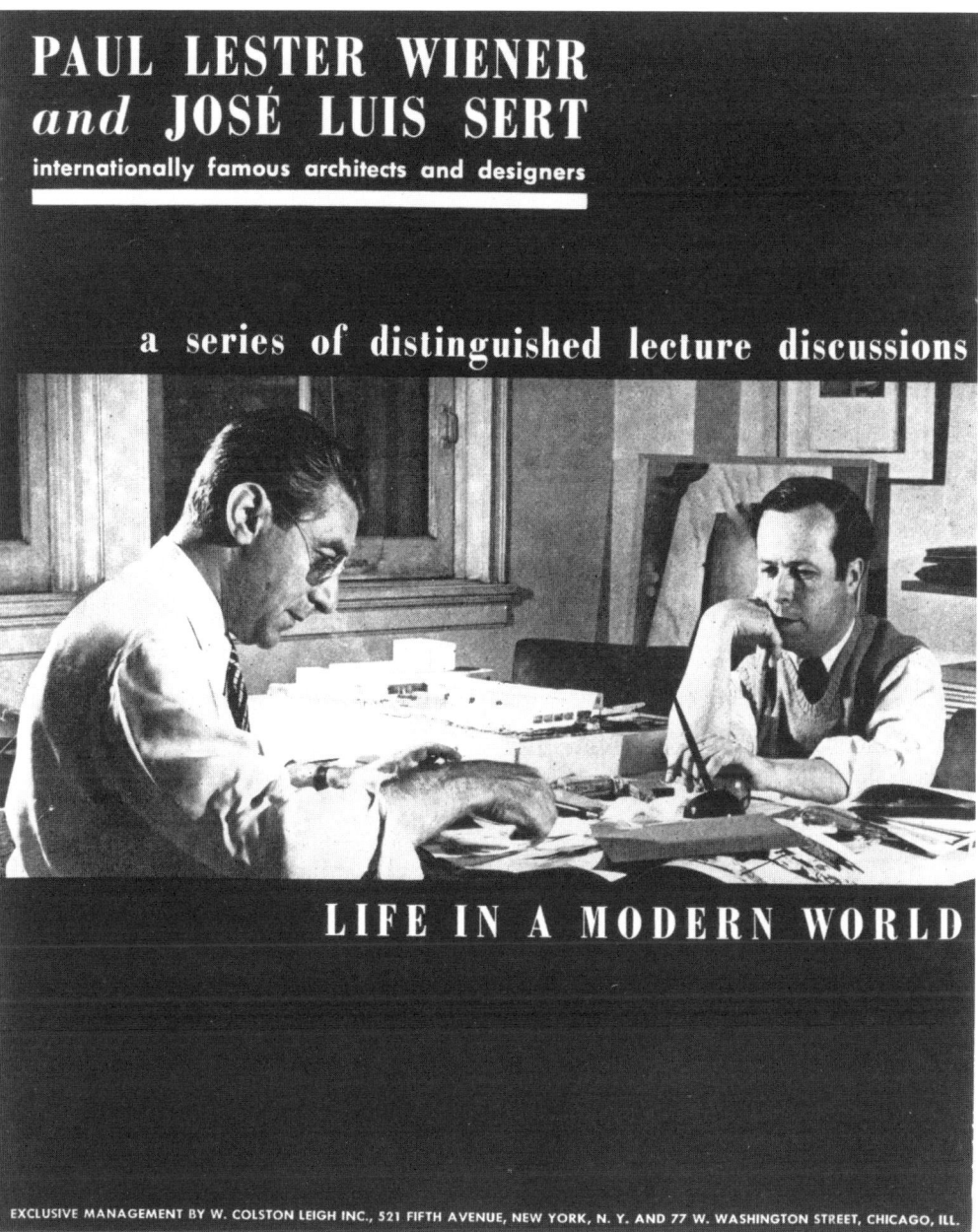

Town Planning Associates brochure showing Wiener and Sert at work, circa 1952.

We do find examples in the past, where the city block was the container of a social structure. An example of this were the "cuadras," or square blocks, of many Latin American cities. These cuadras had a big patio in their center. This patio was used by the community of neighbors, and it served as a gathering place for young and old, functioning as a recreation area, play lot, and public park or community club.

But, as land values increased, every square foot became precious and had to produce the greatest possible revenue. Buildings piled up higher, and the once-sunny patios were replaced by rear apartments, service alleys, and small ventilation shafts. As overcrowding increased, community life became practically impossible. Neighbors had no place to meet, and children lacked open areas to play in. Schools and play lots appear only in scattered spots unrelated to any all-over plan. Distances to get to these places of recreation and community life are much too long, and the roads that lead to them are crossed by traffic arteries.

The possibilities of neighbor meeting neighbor have persistently decreased as the social structure of the city cracks up. We have to realize that houses, offices, shops, factories, and streets distributed without order or plan cannot make a good community* and will never shape better citizens. A community of no matter the size or type, has to facilitate contacts between people; this is one of its most essential functions. These human contacts mean a free exchange of ideas. Without this free exchange of ideas our culture, which is a city-made culture, would never have developed.

Seen from the air, our cities lack shape and size; they appear amorphous and inhuman; they have no elements of measure related to the human scale. The chaos that exists down below is clearly apparent from above. Yet, if we observe nature, we will see that all the elements around us are governed by certain principles of measure and scale. Man is born with a sense of measure or develops it very early in life. It is part of human nature which is antagonistic to the infinities which men cannot grasp. The twenty-four-hour solar cycle governing our lives imposes a scale and measure in the plans of our cities.

In recent city developments the most elementary human needs have been overlooked. Whenever housing projects are carried out, no effort is made toward organizing a better life for the community, and governments and cities think only in terms of shelter. As far as planning is concerned, the most elementary principles of modern city planning are ignored. As a result, many of the new housing groups are fast becoming obsolete blighted areas. We have to approach the problems of housing today from a broader angle and consider them part of city planning. If we do this, we will solve many problems at once, and we will get the proper relationship and integration between the residential areas in a city and all the other sectors of the urban complex.

If we take this broad approach we will see that there is a need in city planning for a *new measure related to man and to the social structure of the community.* This measure should be the expression of a better way of living, one more adapted to the needs and conditions of our times.

---

* "A community—any circle of people who live together, who belong together so that they share, not this or that particular interest, but a whole set of interests wide enough and complete enough to include their lives."—Robert M. MacIver [MacIver was an American sociologist and professor at Columbia University, 1929-50]

View of La Candelaria (Old City), Bogotá.

Cities in the past had a measure or scale closely related to the conditions and ways of living of their inhabitants. The walking distances were determining factors in the sizes of the neighborhoods or districts where the daily activities developed; the homes, the meeting places, the church, the public square were close together. The size of the city as a whole was of course also limited by the capacity of the immediate region to nourish its population and to provide for its most elementary needs.

Mechanized means of transportation, new means of production and food conservation, etc., have transformed the scale of cities, and our sprawling communities of today no longer have any relation to the human scale. The nineteenth century saw this growth of cities as an expression of economic prosperity, which was then considered synonymous to happiness, but as it is a recognized fact today that a complete disregard for human needs has made many of the cities bad places to live in, this has resulted in the decay and blight of large residential sections within the city. These sectors have been vacated by the families that move out to the suburbs, attracted by the promises of a more human environment.

A similar movement from the center to the suburbs is taking place in industry, and as a result, taxation increases outside the city and decreases within its limits. One day, very soon, this movement will have to be reversed, but this will be possible only if a better life can be organized inside the large cities close to the central sectors. This fact has only been recently recognized, but since the last war, the efforts on the part of the planners and authorities in trying to find means to improve living conditions by redevelopment of blighted areas have increased. Measures such as new zoning legislation, new building codes, the creation of city-planning commissions, and the establishment of master plans governing the development of cities are also being adopted, so as to avoid the repetition of the past mistakes that are consequences of the laissez-faire policy.

In spite of some good intentions, what has been done today is very little, though significant. No efforts should be spared from now on, to do much more about city planning. Many countries, especially those that are being industrialized since the last war, are still in a position to avoid the mistakes that have led the more developed countries to the difficult conditions prevailing in their urban areas today. On the other hand, it is in the more developed countries where urban conditions present the greater problem, and planners in these countries have further advanced the studies of how to cope with these critical conditions and would be more careful to avoid the repetition of errors. The younger and less developed countries could use this knowledge and experience to their own immediate benefit, but they are not aware of the dangers of unplanned growth. In their turn, the more experienced technicians would find in these less-developed countries an easier testing ground for their theories.

The neighborhood unit principle will find a wider application in those cities of recent growth where land patterns are less frozen and land assembly is easier. Any new master plan for a city will require a new street pattern that is properly classified so as to separate high-speed traffic from slow traffic and service streets, establishing also a pedestrian network separated from that of motorized traffic. Once the main arteries of the city have been established, the remaining streets will result after the residential sectors and the neighborhood units that compose them have been determined.

Neighborhood planning is the "control of disintegrating elements, the affirming of social values, and the sustaining of the cooperative community."* The neighborhood unit is, by definition, an area where safe and good residential conditions are established. No through streets should cross such areas. This permits pedestrian circulation within them to be safe and easier. These neighborhood units will reinstate the realm of the pedestrian, and open areas of natural beauty, properly landscaped, will then be found near the homes. Man's natural environments, which were banned from the cities for greater benefit of short-sighted land speculators, should be reestablished.

This problem set before the city planners is that of organizing residential sectors within the city where man will find not only shelter but something more: *real homes in the full meaning of the word, places of abode, peace, and rest*. Yet homes, no matter how good they may be, need appropriate surroundings, *an environment congenial to man*. There, natural elements such as plants, trees, water, sun, shade, light, and air should be found near those homes. But both these factors, homes and congenial environment, could not provide *the proper home habitat* if community life cannot find a proper and more stimulating setting in the *neighborhood community services* which really constitute the extension of those homes and their ties to the neighborhood and, through it, to the city as a whole. These community services of the neighborhood are the

---

* E. G. S. Elliot, "Neighborhood Units," *Town Planning Review* (June 1935): 251.

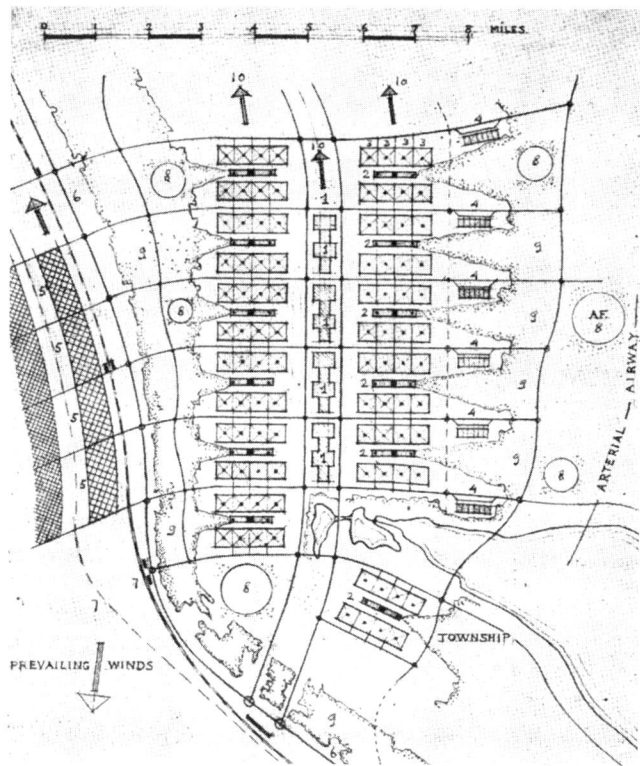

Sert, diagrammatic plan for a city of 960,000, with twelve neighborhood units, 1944.

Theoretical pattern of a neighborhood unit mentioned by Sert, from *Town Planning Review,* June 1935, 251. Drawing by Walter Baumgarten.

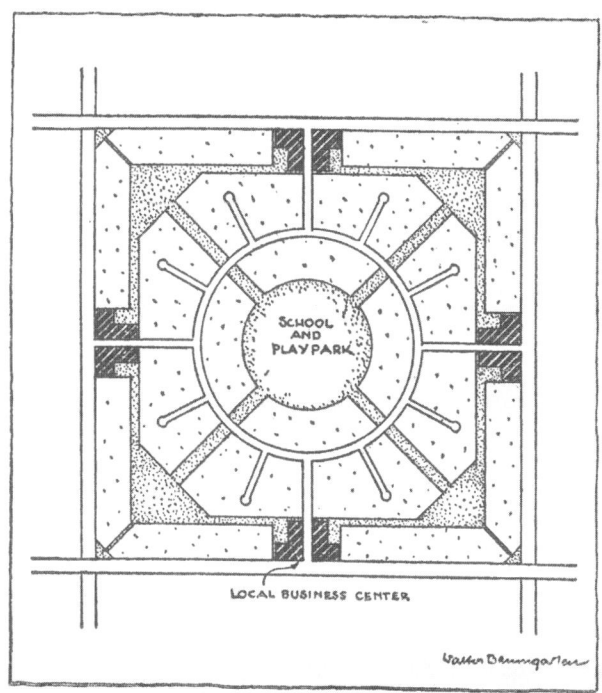

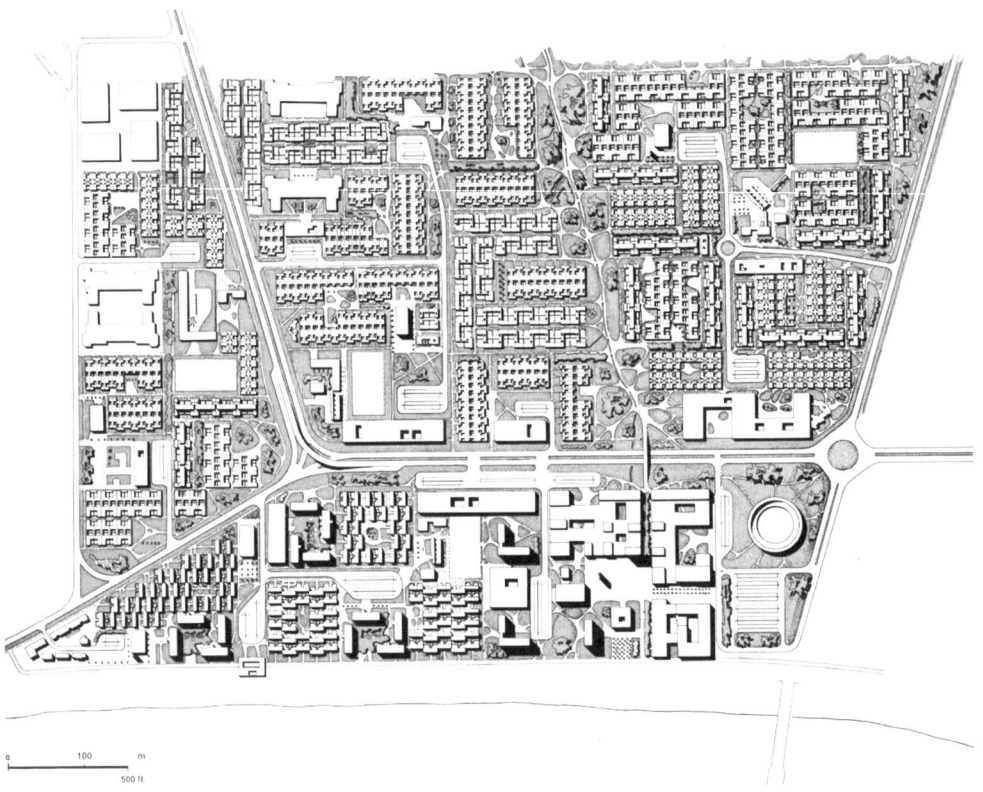

Town Planning Associates, Chimbote Masterplan, 1948. The plan introduced lowrise courtyard houses as the basic housing element of the neighborhood unit, which then became widely influential in Peruvian low-cost housing and had extensive influence elsewhere outside of South America.

framework and container of the social life, the meeting places of young and old, the kindergartens, schools, play fields, shops, churches, and clubs. It is there that the neighborhood spirit develops, is consolidated and expands. In them the pride in the community is born. This will happen when people come to realize the advantages of living together in organized, well-planned communities.

The community services are what make the neighborhood; they provide the meeting places for the community, and they constitute its core. The success or failure of such neighborhoods will greatly depend on the planning and organization of these services. A bad plan, or the wrong placement of the service buildings in regard to homes and roads may make these services unworkable. There are many different opinions on how these services should work, but there is a general agreement on the kind and number of services required. These are:

> The community center or community club
> The elementary school
> A small public library
> A kindergarten and day nursery
> Places for open-air recreation and play fields
> A church
> Local stores, consumer cooperative, small market, movie theater, garages,
> service stations, laundry, repair shops, public parking areas.

It is too often assumed that the core or center of the neighborhood unit is the elementary school, when it should really be the community club or community center, as it is there that neighbors will meet more frequently and the neighborhood spirit will take shape. The two buildings can sometimes be combined for economy and to make greater use of such facilities as auditoriums, canteens, and administrative offices, etc. "The public schools are serving as community centers in many places, and educational leaders point out the special justification for this in that the schools belong to the whole community and because they are located close to the homes of the people. . . . The schools should be integrated into the life of the community—[with] wider use of the school plant. Whether the school is either the or a center of activity depends on local conditions."*

The services, in general, can be grouped in two different sections: (a) the social services and (b) the commercial buildings. Several social service buildings, such as a community center, elementary school, kindergarten, library, and small health center can be successfully combined in one architectural group around an enclosed or open area that can be used as a gathering place in special occasions for local celebrations. If this area is enclosed, the whole group of buildings can be controlled by one caretaker living on the site. This makes the upkeep easier and reduces maintenance costs.

The commercial group of buildings includes the shops and stores, laundry, movie theaters, garage, etc., all of a utilitarian type. These buildings will produce an income. It is advisable to

---

* Arthur Hillman, *Community Organization and Planning* (New York: Macmillan, 1950).

make use of simple structures such as a roof on posts of a certain size... that will permit easy modular additions as more space for such shops is required. These buildings should be located on the periphery near the main roads. Ample parking space has to be provided for these shops.

These commercial groups can be used by several neighborhood units, and many authors recommend that they be placed near the crossroads or intersections of the main street. But it seems more advisable not to crowd these intersections and, rather, to place these groups along the main arteries at certain distances from such crossings, giving them easy access from the service roads running along the sides of the main arteries. The social service group, on the contrary, will be better placed toward the center of the neighborhood. As a rule, these community buildings will be managed by the community association of the neighborhood.

They should be light, flexible structures, because in time the allocation of space may have to change, as when new programs for the use of these buildings are adopted. We should consider that there is no perfect or final program for such services and that continued revisions and modifications will be required as experience teaches the neighbors and educators the lessons that can be learned only once such a community life has been started.

The architect can use simple means, such as pure colors and varied textures, to enliven these buildings and make them look attractive. Some school buildings of recent date constructed in Hoddesdon (England) present these characteristics and offer a good example that should be followed. The need for a residential unit or neighborhood within cities, where a more satisfactory way of living can be organized, has been widely recognized and accepted by city planners in every country. What such neighborhood units should consist of—their size or area, the population, the density (or ratio of people to land), the type of the buildings (one-

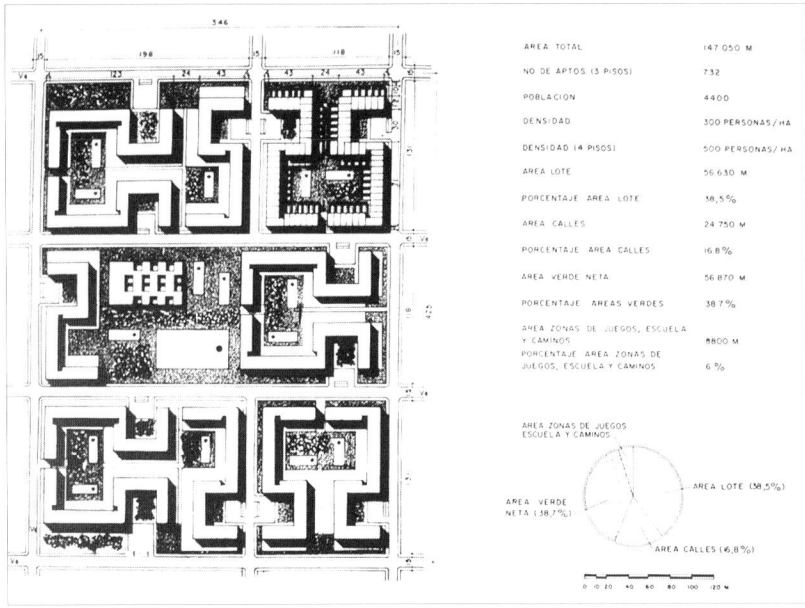

Town Planning Associates, part of neighborhood sector showing provision of communal services, Bogotá Masterplan, 1950-53, used by Sert in his urban design pedagogy at the Harvard Graduate School of Design.

family houses or apartments), the private gardens vs. community parks, the social service buildings and their types, etc.—have long been objects of long debates.

There have been many attempts to establish general programs for these neighborhood units to determine density of population, type of houses and apartments, standards for community buildings and parks, etc., of universal application or use. But after many efforts and good intentions, we have to recognize today that though the general principles can be of worldwide acceptance, there is not a precise program applicable to all countries and climates. It is even difficult to find one that can apply anywhere in the same country. We will easily understand this if we consider the differences in the standard of living of the populations, affecting their customs and purchasing capacity, and those of the climate, topography of the site, and the particular conditions of the city where this site is located, etc. All these factors will be decisive in shaping the plans of the neighborhood units.

The wide acceptance of the neighborhood unit principle, and the recognition of its usefulness, has multiplied the studies for such units in the most varied parts or the world under completely different conditions. But what has actually been built is only a very small part of what has been planned. Efforts to carry out such neighborhood unit plans are increasing everywhere, and it can be useful today to show some studies made to solve this important problem.

Let us start by considering different types of housing. We can distinguish the more urban types developed in Central and Western Europe shortly after the First World War. The federal housing projects started in the U.S.A. under the Roosevelt administration and were greatly influenced by the Central European types. We can compare these with the English garden city types and those of the "Greenbelt" communities in the U.S., and also the ones designed in later years for suburban developments both in America and Europe. It is interesting to note that many of the less developed countries in Latin America, North and South Africa, and the Near East have undertaken large housing schemes since the end of the last war.

Some of these housing programs were large enough to have permitted the development of complete neighborhood units, and we could have many more finished examples to show today. Unfortunately, governments and cities had not at that time established master plans that could have integrated these residential sectors into the larger framework of the community, so the majority of examples of such housing schemes lack community services of any kind. They do not, as a rule, dispose of enough open space to be able to organize play lots and play fields, and the plan does not lend itself to community pattern, as this way of living has not been the determining factor of such plans. These housing schemes have only taken as a basis the replacement of slums with better and healthier types of dwellings, without trying to [impose] a new pattern of community life that would establish a closer relationship between people.

Since the end of World War II, however, there has been a wider recognition of the need for town planning, as reconstruction of large areas had to be undertaken. Also, many previously undeveloped countries are coming of age and [moving] into a new industrialized phase of their existence. Planning on a larger scale is needed practically everywhere, and neighborhood units will be built not only in the very advanced countries, where the theory started and where the first types were tested, but also in other less developed regions. That is why, we believe, it is important to clarify the concept of neighborhood unit at this time.

As is usually the case, mistakes are made in the first attempts to apply these new theories, and the *least developed countries have tried to follow the few existing models too closely.* They do not consider whether all types are applicable to the varying local conditions and that these conditions may determine entirely new patterns that they often overlook. As we adapt housing, social services, landscaping, and roads to the various building methods, standards of living, customs, etc., of each region or city in question, important changes will have to be made.

We use the terms "region or city" in this case in reference to country because today, architecture and city planning are following international trends, and these trends are affected only by such conditions as climate, materials, etc., and not by national, traditional, or historical styles. This is the natural consequence of the new systems of communications that have brought the various countries and people closer together, exchanging persons, goods, words, and images, and tending to level the differences that have been established by physical barriers.

The movement toward internationalism in architecture and city planning is part of a general trend. But as far as the community is concerned, we should not forget that our shelter is still tied to the soil and the soil is conditioned by climate and other unchangeable factors. Besides, people still have different ways of life and customs, etc., and although these are open to changes and improvements, a considerable length of time will be required for these changes to operate. Meanwhile, these people need shelter, not only in the form of isolated houses, but shelter as part of an organized community, where health, education, etc., should be part of the program.

The two previous statements are not contradictory because we must consider actual conditions against the background of future trends. *We should find flexible formulas determining community plans that will vary as standards of living change and progress. We must plan for better living today and also for a better tomorrow. Life cannot stop to wait for our plans, it will continue to flow. So the task of the planner is not to try to adapt life to his plans but to design his plans to fit the changing patterns of living.*

In trying to plan a community, the city planner may be faced with very difficult problems; it will be his duty to analyze and consider local conditions carefully in each case. He must study them, not only in view of what they are today but of what they should and could be tomorrow. His plan, if it is a good plan, will take into consideration all progressive changes and growth, not only physical growth but also spiritual growth. *The planner's community should care for both mind and body; it shall shape better people, and in this sense the neighborhood unit, which is the smaller expression for a community structure, has an important task to perform.*

It is a well-established fact that places such as schools, clinics, hospitals, sports fields, etc., where great numbers of people will have to find attendance, must have a certain scale or size related to their functions. This size may vary considerably, but it will always remain within certain limits. If the structure is too small it will not fulfill the social need of bringing people together, and [the] results [will be] too costly; if it is too large it becomes uncontrollable, and rigid rules must be imposed. Generally, these rules tend to make it inhuman. *The correct measure or scale is an all-important factor in city planning as it is in any community structure, and it must be carefully considered when designing a neighborhood unit.*

What is a desirable size of a neighborhood unit? What area should it cover? How large should its population be? As previously stated, there is no general rule permitting us to give precise figures, but it is recognized that the area of the neighborhood unit should be such that all distances within it can be easily kept within walking scale. One quarter of a mile is often given as the maximum measure from any home to the main community services, such as the elementary school or club. A time limit of fifteen minutes has also been taken as a measure. Climate is of course an important consideration, and walking conditions are different in warm, temperate, or cold areas. Supposing the neighborhood unit is located on a steep mountain slope, the area would have to be smaller and distances kept shorter. Walking conditions can be made easier by protection from sun and rain by trees and other means. The area covered by the neighborhood unit should not be uselessly increased, but a certain population is required to maintain the community services, i.e., kindergartens, schools, clubs, play fields, shops, churches, etc. This population will have to vary according to the paying capacity per capita, which is in direct relation to the standard of living of the population.

On the other hand, in poorer countries the governments, local and national (federal), have to realize that such community services must be provided regardless of the paying capacity of the population involved. Governments and cities should consider this question as one of general welfare, affecting the country and the city as a whole. Wherever possible, the population should pay for these services, but since these services are required, the governments, national or local, will have to provide for their establishment and maintenance, and, in this respect, consider three types of neighborhood units. Those are—

1. **The population is able to maintain and pay for these services.**
2. **The population is only partly able to absorb the costs and needing government subsidy.**
3. **The population is entirely unable to absorb the costs, consequently needing full government subsidy.**

The majority of the world's population belongs to this last group, and these are the groups that require more careful study because *it is precisely these more destitute populations that most need those social services.* It is also among these poorer people that much more can be accomplished by developing neighborhood contacts and promoting group relations. These social services will help to lift the spiritual and physical level of these underprivileged groups. Architecture and planning can help solve this problem, but great ingenuity should be exercised in providing homes, social services, and an agreeable environment for these people. *The means being very scarce, it is the planner's duty to make the most he can of them. Consequently, he should design the neighborhood units so that they can be built economically, operate efficiently, and be maintained with small expense.*

The size of neighborhood unit—population: The previous consideration should help us answer some questions. The size of the neighborhood unit will be determined in each case by local conditions. The population should be large enough to maintain community services, because without these the neighborhood spirit cannot develop. But if the group is too large, contacts are difficult and we would be dealing with a residential sector rather than with a neighborhood. The more generally accepted population figures range from 5,000 to 10,000 inhabitants; the lowest go down to 3,000 and the highest up to 12,000.

Area and density: Once we accept a given population figure as the most desirable, the area over which we spread this population must be our next consideration. This poses the very debatable question of density or ratio of people to land. Here again, there is no ideal desirable density, but there are limits both up and down the scale. The density should not be so high as to create overcrowding, depriving the people of necessary space and resulting in congestion of roads and services at certain times, such as peak hours. Then again, it should not be so low as to create dispersion, increasing walking distances, making contacts difficult, overextending utilities and roads and consequently raising their costs, and making maintenance too high. Through careful planning of accesses and roads to take on the peak-hour loads and with good elevator systems for apartment buildings, high densities may work. But the plan should take all these factors into consideration and also have high buildings so placed as to absorb the excess density. This will result in a greater amount of open space for community use that the high buildings would help to liberate.

We do not want to convey by this that all buildings should be high or that they should be low; as a rule, it seems more desirable to combine high and low types in the same neighborhood. The ratio will have to be determined in each case when establishing the program. It has often been stated that low buildings are more favorable for families with young children, and apartment buildings more appropriate for single people or families with few children or grown-up children. We believe that the arguments have been too one-sided, and if apartment buildings are properly planned and combined with low houses, the program can serve the needs of any type of population. It is more difficult to make use of apartment buildings housing populations of a lower cultural level accustomed to living in semi-rural conditions, but these populations will require special types of housing anyhow.

The density figures given as desirable in many books and magazines are, as a rule, low. They range from 20 persons to the acre to about 100 (50 to 250 to the hectare), acceptable only up to 200 in central sectors of large cities (500 to the hectare). Any figure under 50 persons to the acre (125 to the hectare) seems too low when considering the neighborhood units inside the city limits, and this density and higher ones can be easily reached, obtaining results that are both good and economical. The 200-persons-to-the-acre density can be very simply attained, especially if apartment buildings are included in the neighborhood. Some recent housing developments in large cities have attained a density of over 400 persons to the acre (1,000 to the hectare). This figure seems to be close to the highest limit.

There has been of late a general tendency to condemn high densities per se. This, we believe, is greatly due to a general reaction against the existing overcrowding in our big cities. This reaction has influenced many city planners, carrying them to other extremes in trying to promote very open, dispersed plans of the so-called garden city type. There is nothing basically wrong with this type of community (apart from its costs) if it is considered as an independent community or as part of a small city, let us say up to 50,000 people. But as soon as we speak in terms of a large city, where such community units constitute the prevailing type, this dispersion factor would be multiplied to such an extent that it would complicate the functioning of the city tremendously by increasing distances and making displacements difficult. This will be the case even if we suppose that every family owns one automobile; this solution as has now been applied in the more developed countries would be, of course, more unfavorable in other parts of the world, where automobile ownership is very limited and people must rely on mass means of transportation. In the United States and Britain, where such plans have met greater acceptance, the ratio of cars to people is higher.

Unfortunately, many countries, where living standards and conditions are quite different from those of the U.S.A. and Britain, have been too ready to copy these types of neighborhoods, and the results shown are not too encouraging. No one can pay for the overextension of utilities and maintain roads that are not justifiable because of the scarcity of automobiles. Experience shows that if we deal with a neighborhood as part of a large city, a certain compactness is desirable because of the cost of land, utilities, and roads, and so as to make the distances between home and work as short as possible. We can figure on net densities of about 250 to 375 people per hectare or 100 to 150 to the acre for patterns of compact row housing. If apartment buildings are used, this density can be increased up to 500 or 750 per hectare, 200 or 300 to the acre. These figures allow the necessary acreage for all types of small community service buildings, play fields, play lots, small parks, peripheral shops, and service streets as can possibly be maintained by the low standards of living of such populations.

It should be here stated that in this study of the neighborhood unit, we are mainly concerned with types of neighborhoods that are more adaptable to the low-income groups and in a special manner to those of the less developed countries. We should not forget that these constitute the vast majority of the world population and present the greatest challenge to the planner. It is also this type of population that is most in need of community services for health, education, and recreation. Also in these vast schemes, the benefits derived from organizing building systems based on mass production, and new methods of construction predicated on repetitive parts, will produce more interesting results.

The choice of examples following this introduction has been made taking this into consideration. The programs and methods of building apply to neighborhood units in different parts of the world and will, as previously stated, vary considerably, but there are a certain number of factors everywhere that will have to be taken into consideration and that can be grouped as follows:

a) **The natural conditions of the site** (unchangeable factors) would impose different types of neighborhoods for cold climates, temperate climates with seasons, tropical and subtropical climates. In each latitude, the climate can vary greatly by such conditions as altitude and proximity to the sea, which will influence the degree of humidity, rainfall, temperatures, etc.

b) **The factors related to the man-made environment—populated areas and their degree of development,** proximity of industry, agricultural areas, etc., and our neighborhood units—will be different if they are part of a rural or agricultural region; a semi-rural area with low land values; a suburban sector where a great amount of land is still available; or a sector inside a city with high land values. These land values, and the property on the land, and the way it has been subdivided will of course greatly facilitate or complicate the task of the planner.

c) **The factors relating to the occupational activities of the populations, their customs, types of families, etc.:** these will also greatly differ if we deal with agricultural sectors or with workers in industry, offices, or shopping districts.

The climate conditions are a very important factor in the determination of the plan. For example, hot tropical or subtropical climates require more space between buildings, special control of fast growing vegetation, protection from the elements, and orientation of all the houses in a certain direction so that they may obtain the best benefits from the prevailing breezes. For those hot climates, community buildings may be extremely simple and in some cases something resembling a shed or large umbrella constituting a light roof structure on posts, leaving many areas open.

For some subtropical rainless regions, such as the southwest coast of South America, where the Humboldt current cools the coastal region, the conditions are very different. Temperatures are moderate and houses can be much closer together, but green areas must be artificially maintained by irrigation. This means that these green areas must be small, forming oases between groups of houses that cluster around them. Private gardens and patios are convenient for these regions, as they can be maintained by tenants, and these result in considerable savings on the part of the city. Low walls give protection to these private gardens and encourage families to become interested in taking good care of them. Other systems may be devised, such as one combining the characteristics of the two previous types. This could be done grouping buildings closer together for easier and more economical utilities but surrounding them with open spaces that would permit circulation of air so that the people can benefit by the prevailing breezes.

In tropical climates, all existing big trees on site should be kept, as they offer very good protection against heat and make pedestrian circulation more agreeable. In the northern climates we find entirely different conditions. There, protection of pedestrians is still important, and in such neighborhood units as the ones now being planned in the redevelopment of the south sector of Chicago, all factors of protection against climate must be carefully considered. In a city where temperatures can be extremely cold in winter and hot in summer, where strong winds prevail, it is especially important to plan for the climate and not try to adapt formulas that may have proven successful in other parts of the world, where conditions are different. If we plan a neighborhood unit we should remember that we want to reestablish the walking custom, within its limits. Many planners tend to overlook this, considering people in those neighborhoods would use the automobile [rather than walk], as is the custom today. If they use the automobile, the climate factors are not so important, but if we want to encourage walking within the new neighborhood units, we should make it as agreeable as possible.

Other factors besides those of climate will, of course, influence the plan of these neighborhoods. For example, we can state in a general way that the suburban types of neighborhood unit will make greater use of one-family houses and private gardens than the more urban types located nearest to the center. The density of population will also be lower in the suburban developments, and a more rural way of life should be encouraged in these neighborhoods. As we come closer to the center of the city the land values are higher and the whole plan must become tighter. The density of population should increase not only because of the higher land values, but also because distances have to be made shorter in these central sectors, [or] otherwise risk having to make the city expand further out, extending distances from work to home, increasing the number street crossings with consequent complications in the transportation system. *Cities, as they are today, are already overextended, and we should not carry this outward movement any further wherever possible.*

We should now consider the neighborhood unit in relation to the city as a whole and stress the importance of the ties that have to bind these units to the civic way of life in a general way, and in a closer way, to other larger units such as community units, boroughs, or residential sectors that are formed by groups of neighborhood units. The neighborhood units are part of the city and as such should have close ties to the city sectors or larger units. These sectors will have more complex services, such as high schools, branches of the public library, small museums, exhibition halls, sport centers, stadiums, gymnasiums, sport fields, large stores, hospitals, churches, etc. Some of these services will be grouped into small civic nuclei that will form the core of these residential sectors. This seems to be the correct approach, because *it is not desirable for the neighborhood unit to be more than it should be, a unit for family relationship, to satisfy the immediate needs of families, especially of children, and to give them greater protection.* This has been clearly defined by saying that the neighborhood unit is "that area which embraces all the public facilities and conditions required by the average family for its comfort and proper development within the vicinity of the dwelling."*

There has been of late a tendency to idealize a semi-rural way of life, more like the one that should develop in a village, as against a more urban or civic way of living. This romantic attitude is especially successful in Anglo-Saxon and Scandinavian countries, and a generation of planners have subscribed to its principles. A reaction against this has started in late years, since the end of World War II, and the younger planners are taking a more healthy and realistic attitude toward this subject. They do not in general condemn the neighborhood unit principle, but they have redefined it, limited its influence, and expressed its real value.

A city should never be a conglomeration of villages or small towns, which is what would happen if too much emphasis is placed on the neighborhood unit, making it practically self-sufficient. Besides, the communal facilities that the neighborhood unit can pay for would never be sufficient for the inhabitants of a large city; in that case it would be more favorable to live in a village and profit from the quiet, in the vicinity of the unspoiled countryside, than to try to create a village within a city. This romantic school of planners wants to promote something between the urban and rural way of life, a neither-city-nor-country product that would, in some ways, resemble suburban developments, the advantages and defects of which we know too well.

To us it seems that the trend should be entirely the opposite one. We should plan compact neighborhood units, some of them very urban in character, real civic landscapes. These units would be grouped into residential sectors, and between these the countryside in all its natural and agricultural beauty could remain unspoiled. In these plans, the civic and rural landscapes would alternate, but between them there would be clear lines of demarcation. In this way we would avoid the depressing effect our suburbs have of spilling over the countryside without any control or plan. There would be a sharp contrast between the rural and the

---

* Clarence L. Perry, *Housing for the Machine Age* (New York: Russell Sage Foundation, 1939).

urban, and each of these residential sectors would have a particular character of its own. This character would be shaped by the special conditions of the site, the standard of living of the population, and also by the type of architecture and planning chosen for the sector as a whole.

Cities of the type would be organic; that is, composed of several parts expressing different functions. No matter how large the city, there would always be a feeling of scale about it, and the scale would be related to man. Automobiles would move along highways of the parkway type, bordered by greenbelts, behind which would lie the well-planned residential sectors providing a humanized environment for the people. *The neighborhood units would be the cells or component parts of these sectors or community units with a population of 30,000 to 60,000,* equivalent to small cities that could afford complete community services and be self-sufficient. This does not mean that larger cities would not exist, but these larger cities would be formed by clusters of these sectors.

The larger cities are a must, because only a large population can stimulate, produce, and maintain activities of specialized character, such as costly cultural, scientific, and recreational organizations where people can learn, specialize in certain kinds of work, and have greater opportunities to meet other people. We should not forget that it is in large centers of populations like these that our modern culture has found its highest expression. In spite of the nuisances of the large cities today, such as overcrowding, excess travel time, etc., people continue to migrate to them in growing numbers.

We have also to avoid making the neighborhood unit an element of segregation, tending to separate certain portions of the population from others and fomenting antagonism between small groups. On the contrary, we should try to attain better understanding between people, and this will be facilitated if the services in the neighborhood unit are properly organized and community living is made as attractive as possible. This is really the main task of the planner in any city, and his plan should be so designed that it will bring people of all levels of life together.

As previously stated, the neighborhood unit can accomplish this only on a family level. But these family contacts are extremely important and sometimes the most difficult. If the neighborhood unit is successful in fulfilling its social program, the residential sector can be easily organized and contacts on the higher level, such as in high schools, large clubs, or sport fields, will be easier to establish and maintain.

The core of the neighborhood unit should have a close tie to the community unit or residential sector; its shopping centers and movie theaters will be constantly used by the neighbors of the smaller units. All these movements of population from the smaller to the larger units will overlap as people from the various sectors congregate. The neighborhood units have no real physical barrier separating them from one another. Classification, if well planned, will only make for an easier flow of communications between them. The cores of the residential sectors should, in turn, be connected with the central core, or "heart of the city." There will be a network of social services extending from the neighborhood unit cores to those in different sectors of the city, all of them linked by parks and roads. This network will be the physical expression of the social structure of the city and of the ties that should hold the different units together.

The street system in the new plans will be a classified one in contrast to the unclassified, outmoded gridiron pattern of the streets of today. The streets bordering the neighborhood units and those feeding the homes and services will be part of this general system, which should be designed to serve the needs of mechanized transportation. The main arteries for rapid traffic or thoroughfare streets will be determined by regional topography and other particular conditions. They will connect the furthest parts of the city with the central sector and lead out into the region, of which the city is only a part. They will establish links to other regions and cities. The through-traffic should use these streets and avenues and not disturb more quiet areas. There should also be other streets establishing links between these avenues. This location will be determined by the shape and size of the community units or sectors. These streets will run along the borders of these sectors but not cross them. Streets of a different character for slower traffic, similar to our shopping or main streets, would feed into these sectors and subdivide them into neighborhood units. Then, other streets will lead on from these commercial streets toward the core of the neighborhood unit and also serve the houses and apartment blocks. These service streets would be designed so that they do not subdivide the neighborhood unit and constitute through streets or shortcuts encouraging speed.

The success of a neighborhood unit may depend greatly on the way it is connected with the rest of the city by a good flow system. The neighborhood unit being only the center of family life, as stated above, the people living there would have to go to work outside of this unit. Theoretically, it would be ideal for people to work right in the neighborhood unit or in the adjacent areas, eliminating the long *traveling to work,* which is a daily waste of time, money, and human energy. But we should not forget that we live in a city because it is a place where great opportunities for any kind of work can be found. We want to have the freedom to choose the type of work we like, and to change our occupation when we please. Besides, several members of a family usually have various occupations and work in different places. Sometimes these places are very far apart. To establish factories or offices near the home would demand the people in that vicinity to work next door; it would tie them to a specific type of work, which may not be the one of their choice. This was possible in the past, when all members of the household helped the head of the family in his workshop. It was simple then, but conditions today do not make it desirable or possible. There is no other alternative but to make the journey to work as easy as we can. We have to measure this journey in terms of time, not distance, met by means both easy and comfortable.

If the service roads in the neighborhood unit and those on its fringes are directly connected with the rapid traffic system, it should be possible to cover long distances on these roads or avenues in a very short time. For a large city, fifteen minutes by automobile or express bus can be considered a desirable time limit. It will not be of much use to try to organize a better family life in the neighborhood unit if we do not solve the system of rapid communications. To enjoy life one must dispose of some free hours each day for recreation and rest. If these hours are taken up by travel from home to work, the majority of the adults in these neighborhood units will not be able to make use of the social and recreational services, which will then benefit only the children and those few members of the community working near their neighborhood.

As cities have expanded, there has been a tendency to study the redevelopment of the central areas so as to bring people back to the city. Many people working in the central sectors of the city are aware that they are losing too much time commuting to the distant suburbs. Transportation to some suburban areas is difficult, so that many suburbanites would be willing to come back to the central sectors to live closer to their work if conditions in these sectors are improved. There are many examples of this in cities that have rapidly expanded during the last years, and where the means of mass transportation have not developed accordingly. People constantly complain of the time and money lost in transportation, and these populations can be very easily persuaded to move into the central sectors of the city after a neighborhood unit system is properly established there.

There are, of course, difficulties and obstacles to carrying out such neighborhood units. These difficulties are all of a different caliber. As a rule, the greatest obstacles are presented by the conditions of the land in central sectors. This land is subdivided and, very often, completely built up. The acquisition of buildings and land and its consolidation offers great difficulties. But to carry out a good plan, the land has to be consolidated. In central areas this means acquisition of many small lots and dealing with the numerous owners and tenants. Long debates follow, and when a satisfactory price cannot be reached, the property must be placed before a jury to determine its fair value. But conditions in cities have become so critical, and blight has spread to such an extent, that what was not possible in the twenties is feasible today.

The City of Chicago offers an example that is especially interesting because of the size of this city and the value of the land. "Chicago has 23 square miles of blighted and slum areas choking the Loop." "About one-fifth of the city's vacant 40 square miles are in tracts of two acres or more and are suitable for residential development. A good portion of this vacant land is blighted, that is, it is tax-delinquent, neglected and unproductive." "Chicago's program to remove blight is being carried out by the Chicago Land Clearance Commission, which was created in 1947 by the Illinois Legislature. The Commission is authorized by law to acquire worn-out neighborhoods, clear them of buildings and sell the sites at use value to private redevelopers for reconstruction."

"Property in a redevelopment site is acquired by the Chicago Land Clearance Commission on fair and equitable terms. Appraisals of the property are made for the Commission by independent appraisers." "Rebuilding of blighted areas furnishes clean and sanitary dwellings within the city and slows down the movement of families to the suburbs. It provides well-designed and self-contained neighborhoods, with schools, parks, and shopping places conveniently located for happier and healthier family life. It creates a highly desirable neighborhood atmosphere."*

The detailed description of the acquisition of such land for the purposes of rearrangement, permitting [us] to build entirely new neighborhood units, is a specialized subject. Other difficulties can be encountered if the new plan demands a modification of the existing city code, and many of these codes are outmoded today and should be revised. As a rule, these modifications can be obtained after some debate. Many cities recognize that they must revise their codes and zoning regulations that were drafted many years ago when conditions were

---

* Chicago Land Clearance Commission, *Chicago's Face Lifting Program* (Chicago, 1952).

totally different from the ones prevailing today. But instead of trying to modify the old codes or establish new ones, it seems wiser to provide a master plan for the city as a whole, and then draft a code that would conform to the plan; otherwise we may impose limitations that will hamper the plan. Once a master plan is established, certain articles of the code will be derived from land use in general: the road system, the community services, the green areas and parks, building heights and regulations, etc.

The new code should, of course, lay special emphasis on the neighborhood unit system. which will be one of the basic elements of any master plan. This is already being done in Chicago and many other cities where any redevelopment, public or private, is being carried out in agreement with the City Planning Commissions. The neighborhood units have to be the healthy cells of the new city, and all redevelopment efforts should be encouraged to carry out some of these units, which may be of an experimental type at the start, as the whole city would later benefit from these experiments.

The neighborhood units, when properly planned as part of the master plan, will be a protection against blight and offer greater stability of land values than would the unplanned neighborhoods. Today, there is no protection against blight, and no matter how good an apartment building or small group of houses are, their character and value in the future will be affected by the ups and downs of their immediate environment. If industry warehousing, unkempt empty land, or blight develops around a new apartment or house, that building, no matter how good in itself, will decrease in value and tenants will soon want to move out to better neighborhoods.

This is not the case when a complete neighborhood unit is built. This area is clearly limited by improved streets that act as a protective belt. It is of course necessary that the neighborhood unit as a whole be maintained in proper shape, and the neighbors' association should take care of this, which is also in their own interests. It is precisely this community of interest that establishes the more enduring guarantee and protection. This is beneficial to the neighborhood as a whole; it affects all the families of the unit. If there are any minority dissensions, these can be overruled by a majority vote. It is not logical to suppose that the majority will work against the interest of the neighborhood.

In dealing with the advantages presented by the neighborhood unit, we would also stress that such groups of housing and services offer an excellent opportunity for the application of modern building methods and the use of mass-produced parts. These modern methods do not offer great advantages unless they are applied to developments of certain size, such as neighborhood units. The application of those methods is not only beneficial but economical, because the number of dwellings is large enough to obtain important price cuts.

In planning these neighborhood units, new systems of construction and mass production should be kept in mind by the team of technicians in charge of such plans, and [the technicians] should work in close touch with the builders that have to carry out the job. The success of the planning and construction of the neighborhood units cannot be ensured unless this work is carried through in the right spirit from beginning to end.

From the initial analytical study and programming done with the help of sociologists, economists, educators, etc., working together with the architects, planners, engineers, and builders, to the drafting of the plans, preparation of the scale models and economic, social, administration, and maintenance studies, there must be perfect coordination. This coordination should continue during the supervision of the work until its total completion. After that, the setting up of the neighborhood committees and the organization of the administrative staff of such a venture will depend on all these factors, and their coordination. The planner-architect is only one important element in such a team.

3

URBAN DESIGN (1953)

This lecture was given October 23, 1953, at the American Institute of Architects Mid-Atlantic Regional conference in Washington, D.C. This was shortly after Sert had been appointed dean of the Harvard Graduate School of Design. The event was organized by Washington planner Louis Justement, and listed speakers included two other architecture deans, George Howe (Yale) and George Holmes Perkins (Penn), as well as former Tennessee Valley Authority planner Tracy Augur, by then director of the Urban Targets Division of the federal Office of Defense Mobilization and a strenuous advocate of postwar urban decentralization for national defense reasons.

This lecture appears to be Sert's first use of the term "urban design," which had been used occasionally by Eliel Saarinen at his Cranbrook Academy of Art. It marks the point when Sert began to attempt to link the ideas that he had advocated in CIAM, about the importance of pedestrian urban life to cultural and political life, to American urban issues. In it, he echoes Lewis Mumford in emphasizing that postwar culture was "a culture of cities, *a civic culture*," as well as Le Corbusier's insistence, derived from earlier Germanic directions, of the need for a three-dimensional approach to urban planning.

EM

I am honored and happy to be here with you tonight. I'm sorry that, because of my work at the Graduate School of Design, I was unable to join this conference before, as the subjects of your seminars—"The Architect and Urban Design and Urban Redevelopment"—are, I believe, especially interesting and timely. At the risk of being repetitious, as I am sure that previous speakers must have made interesting comments on the subject, I should like to make some comments of my own on the architecture of the city. Washington is one of the few cities with an architecturally planned center. It is a civic city, designed and built by men of foresight and courage. It is a well-chosen place for such talks. Here we can appreciate the importance of the civic in architecture, of having buildings related to one another and to the open spaces around them, conceived and built in a planned environment. This, it seems to me, should be one of the highest aspirations of both architects and city planners.

We hear very frequent and justified critical comments on life in cities—their inhuman scale, the traffic congestion, the air pollution, the overcrowding, etc.—all adding up to a serious case against the city and a civic way of life. By contrast, we are presented with the better living conditions in the suburbs and more rural areas.

Reacting to these conditions, the last generation of planners has tried to solve the problems posed by the city by turning their backs on what we can call the city proper.[1] There has been much more suburbanism than urbanism. All means have been devised to get away from the city as an undesirable place to live in, bad for children and bad for grown-ups—the children get run over, the grown-ups get drunk. [It's] a place you should leave as soon as you finish your day's work—get out of it as fast and as far as you can.

As a result of these trends in city planning, and the previous failure of both planners and architects of academic "beaux arts" background to consider the altered conditions of our lives due to the radical changes brought to our cities by the industrial revolution, civic architecture declined and civic design has been practically forgotten.

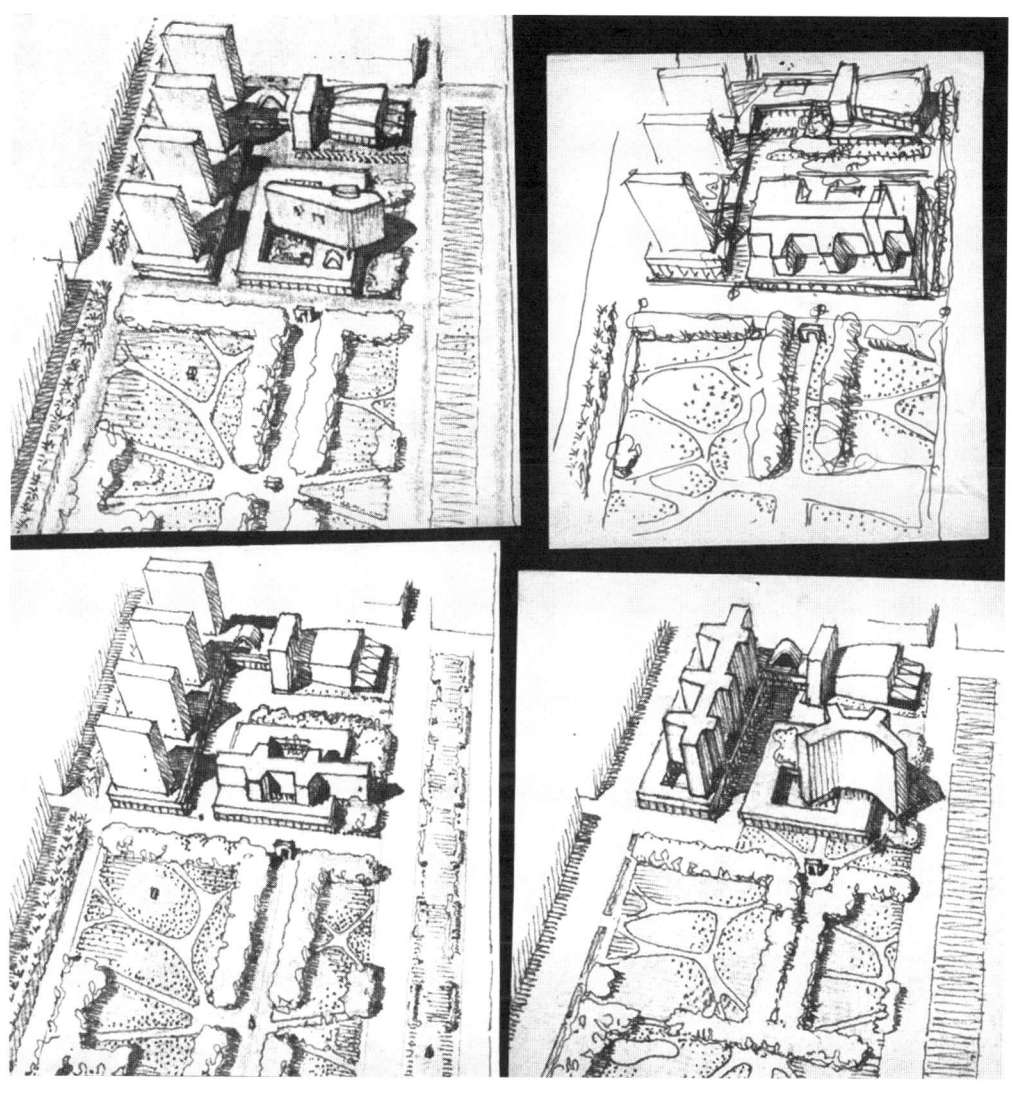

Town Planning Associates, sketches of alternatives for a mixed-use development for Exposition Park, Lima, 1947, influenced by Rockefeller Center in New York as well as Le Corbusier's unbuilt works.

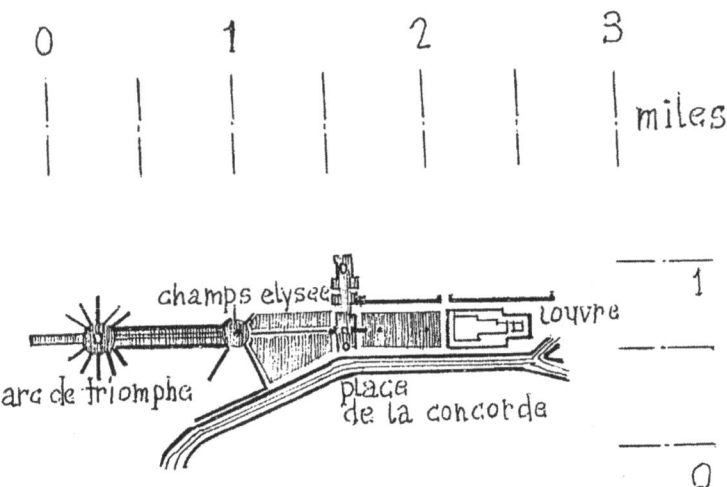

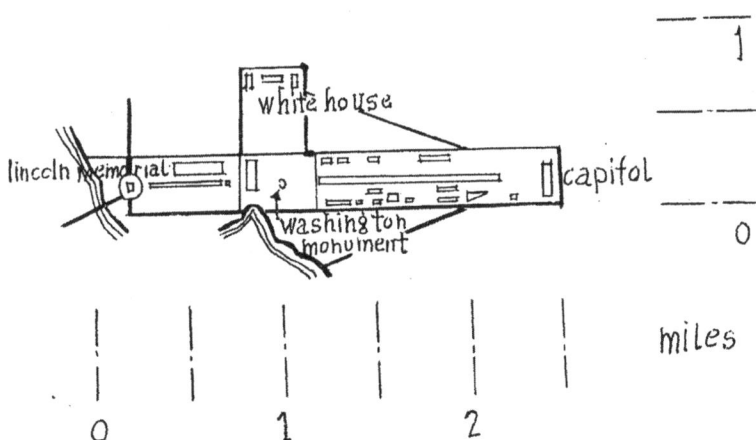

Class presentation, same-scale analysis drawings of Paris and Washington, D.C., by Harvard GSD student Irving Weiner, from Sigfried Giedion with José Luis Sert and Eduard F. Sekler, "The Human Scale: Advanced Seminar for the Master's Class," spring term 1958, fourth meeting, February 26, 1958.

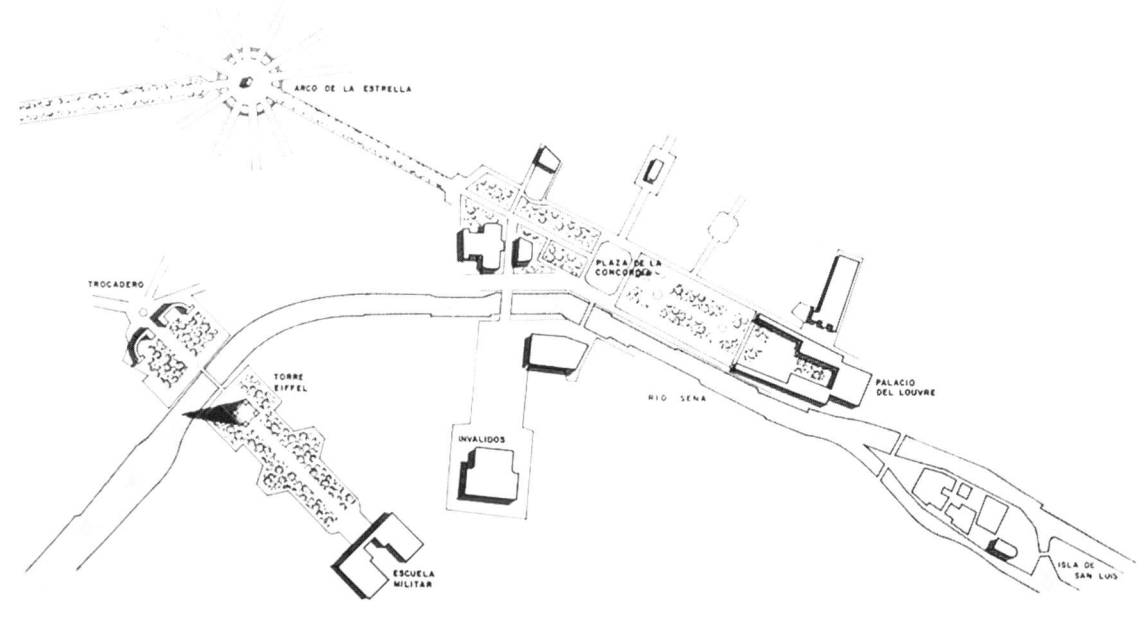

Town Planning Associates, plan of central Paris showing monumental spaces and buildings, 1958, from Town Planning Associates, *Plan Piloto de la Habana*, 1958.

Figures indicate that a great number of cities in this country have now reached maturity. The explosive growth period seems to have given place to more normal, slower growth; the attitude of the people toward their cities has changed lately. They have become conscious that bigger does not necessarily mean better, that it takes more than size and population to make a beautiful city. It is time to pause and reflect.

One of the greatest challenges for architects is the carrying out of the large civic complexes: the integration of city planning, architecture, and landscape architecture, the building of a *complete environment.* This is a vast and ambitious task.

We should be aware of that fact and of all the barriers and limitations that lie in between—such as inflated land values, great vested interests, etc. But, on the other hand, it is increasingly evident that, as conditions in central areas of cities become worse, these same vested interests will eventually recognize that drastic changes will result in benefits to the city as a whole and will help to stabilize and protect land values. The moment to plan has come.

As far as the architect is concerned, we should recognize today that the architectural housecleaning of the twenties and thirties, which did away with the use and misuse of "historic styles," was only a good start in a long race *and that contemporary architecture as a style is still in its beginnings;* that the search for a more complete architectural vocabulary, a more satisfactory architectural expression, should continue; that the development of such a style is not the job of a few men—no matter how talented they are—but, as it has always been in the past, both in architecture and city planning, *the laborious result of the persistent creative efforts of several generations.*

I am talking here of style in the broadest and truest sense of the word, as when it is applied to Gothic, Romanesque, or Baroque, for instance, rather than the sense in which fashion people use it, where it can be one man's profession to be a "stylist."

Architects should decide, together with the city planners, to invade the no-man's-land of civic design. It is a joint job that is required—a teamwork job, where both architects and city planners need the advice and the technical help of many other specialists.

I call this field a no-man's-land because contemporary architecture and planning have not developed in it, and it offers no really full-size example of a complete civic complex that can give us a picture of an entire civic environment where architecture is at its best, in true relation to open areas and traffic networks that can be shown as examples of what the city centers of our time can be.

Up to now, contemporary architecture has produced at best a few scattered good examples of isolated buildings. But much of the more recent work—like that of the twenties, which I had an opportunity to review in Europe after the last war—will be absorbed by an overpowering, hostile environment: the chaotic streets, the creeping blight and slums of our cities. I saw what were once sensational buildings, which made very good magazine pages in the twenties and thirties, now decayed and looking very poor in form and spirit. In no way could these be considered a satisfactory expression of our times.

They look primitive and crude, no matter how functional. They have the merit of a new start, a great transformation in architecture, a break with the past. They have historical interest but, in many cases, no emotional qualities.

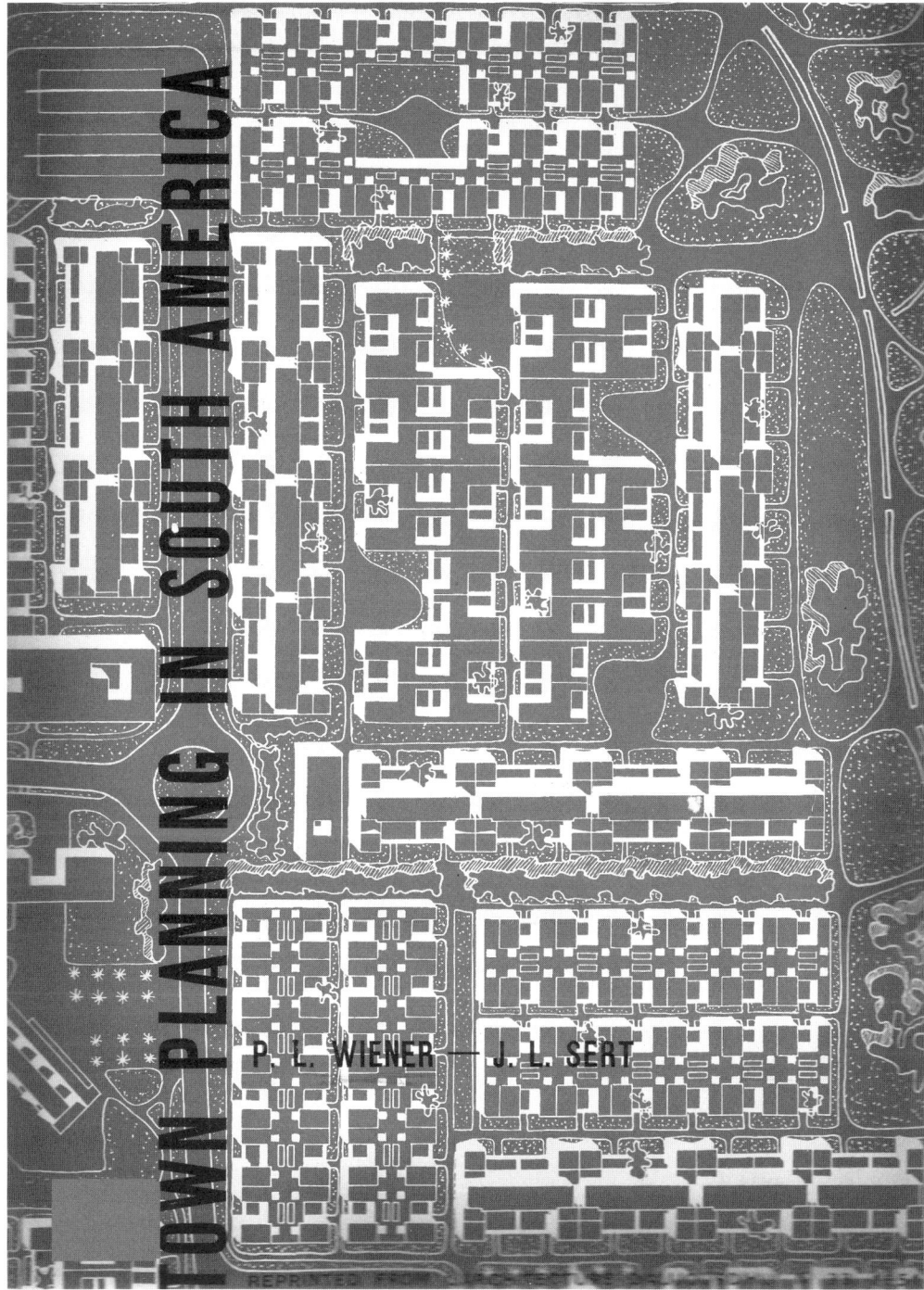

Cover of P. L. Wiener and J. L. Sert, "Town Planning in South America," *L'architecture d'aujourd'hui* 33 (1951), showing the proposed *tapis urbain* (urban fabric) of lowrise courtyard houses for Chimbote.

We should understand that functionalism does not necessarily mean that only the functional has a right to exist: the superfluous is part of our system—it is as old as man. Let us not forget that man decorated the roofs of his cave dwellings before he knew how to build a roof. Why not use elements that are not strictly functional if they do not conflict with function—and make buildings more beautiful?

But the value of great architecture and city planning—a great civic complex—lies in order, classification; a true relationship of space and form, in light. . . . The whole resulting in harmony, which has the same basis and roots of the natural structures in the world around us—minerals, plants, animals, and man. For in all works of art, man has to find part of himself.

Man has put most of himself in the cities. They are his greatest achievement. In them his effort and his spirit are concentrated. Fly over vast continents, as we do today, and imagine cities disappearing; what would remain as an expression of our culture? This culture of ours is a culture of cities, *a civic culture.* It is in the central areas of cities where the landscape is really a man-made landscape that the past shows many examples of civic beauty; civic landscapes sometimes built in the course of centuries, where city planning and architecture are at their best. No isolated building can compete with them. They are a miracle repeated through the ages—the Acropolis, the Piazza San Marco, the Place de la Concorde, etc.

Why should we not today, with more means at hand and the same ancestral need for humanly scaled meeting places, build our new civic centers? Let city planners consider their role incomplete if some of them, at least, do not become physical planners in the full sense of the word, with a broad, three-dimensional approach. Let the architects be ambitious enough to search the means of solving one of the biggest and most difficult problems of our times—the rehabilitation of the central sectors of the hearts of our cities.

If we believe in our times and in the great possibilities of modern techniques, if we believe in the vitality and power of this great country and in a better future, the miracle may happen . . . . and the centers of our great cities may become places of beauty—a proud testimony of our times.

4

ARCHITECTURE AND THE VISUAL ARTS (1954)

This text appeared in the *Harvard Foundation for Advanced Study and Research Newsletter* (December 31, 1954). Sert had been closely involved with the art world since his years as an avant-garde CIAM architect in Barcelona in the 1930s. When in exile in Paris in 1936 he met the American sculptor Alexander Calder, and he commissioned him to design a "Mercury Fountain" for his Pavilion of the Spanish Republic for the 1937 Paris Exposition. This work was installed adjacent to the first exhibition of Pablo Picasso's *Guernica*. This successful collaboration of modern art and architecture in the service of anti-fascism set a pattern for Sert, who immigrated to New York in 1939, staying at the Calders' Connecticut farmhouse after his arrival. During the war, Sert was part of a circle of émigré artists in New York, and after the war he continued these friendships.[1] The artists included Joan Miró, who painted a mural for Skidmore, Owings & Merrill's Terrace Plaza Hotel in Cincinnati (1946) while staying in Sert's New York apartment in 1948, and for whom Sert designed his first work in Spain since 1939, the Miró Studio in Palma de Mallorca (1953). Sert was also close to James Johnson Sweeney, whom he met when Sweeney was a Museum of Modern Art curator in 1939 and with whom he wrote *Antoni Gaudí* (New York: Praeger, 1960), the first major historical reconsideration of the now world-renowned Catalan architect.

EM

I am new to Harvard, and I beg you to forgive me if I talk to you about things you already know and if I'm not too accurate in expressing my thoughts. Looking at things freshly and from another point of view may help, and I may perhaps say some things that have not been said before.

My first interest in life was painting, and from that interest I went to architecture and city planning. My work was always related to the visual arts. The people interested in the visual arts are many in this world, and I think that those who became designers, architects, city planners, or landscape architects are mainly drawn from that group of people interested in the visual arts. This means that, when we choose our students—and we do this as carefully as we can—we take into special consideration their abilities in the field of visual arts. This is sometimes difficult to do because many colleges don't teach those fields as we would like them to. When the girls and boys coming to the graduate school are not prepared in the field of visual arts, it makes work more difficult for them and their studies longer in duration. Four years is a long enough time, as it is, to devote to graduate study—and this is particularly true for those students drafted into military service.

If Harvard is interested in turning out the best possible architects, city planners, and landscape architects, I would like the university to view all the possibilities for making studies shorter, and I would like to get the help of the alumni in this matter, so that our plans can become a reality. To do this we need a very good basic preparation in the visual arts. I know that is not easy, but there are systems today, and those systems have been tried.

I should like to get more students from Harvard College than we are getting now. Last year only 20 percent of our students came from the college. The faculty of design would like to make that 20 percent from Harvard College a 50 percent. But we must confess that there are

Sert, Joan Miró studio, Mallorca, Spain, 1955. Sert's first commission in Spain after going into exile in 1939.

no courses offered in visual design that would give the students in the college the right preparation for entering the School of Design and gaining a degree in the shorter time necessary. Our objective is to have courses given in the college that will prepare the students so that their senior year there would also be their first year in the Graduate School of Design—following which, in three years they would obtain the master in architecture degree, or, in two years, the master in city planning or in landscape architecture. As it is now, the students need four years in the college and four full years after their college preparation is completed.

We are handicapped by this difficulty, because other schools can give degrees in a shorter time—and today the time element is tremendously important for the young people. So we should very much like to get Harvard College to establish the necessary courses in the field of the visual arts, which would give the students a basic preparation permitting them to enter the Graduate School of Design in their senior year.

We also believe that these courses in the visual arts would not be only for the students in the Graduate School of Design but would have a much broader interest. This would help in more than one way because, if instruction in the visual arts were available to people besides those going to the graduate school, not only would we get better architects and better students in the Graduate School of Design, but also many people in other professions would have a greater understanding and a broader appreciation of the work of architects than they have today. We believe that this visual education is tremendously important: we don't say that it should compete with other means of education, but it should be there, besides those other means. We also believe and want to emphasize in the faculty of design the need for means of visualization—means of training people to see—which could really shorten our courses. These could actually give people, in a shorter amount of time, an instruction which takes longer to acquire if it depends on merely the printed or spoken word. By that I mean all means of visualization, such as scale models, good collections of colored slides, movies, etc. We have today wonderful means at hand which did not exist fifty years ago. I don't consider myself so old, yet I have seen the movies come into their own. I have seen the illustrated magazine cover the world and become tremendously important as a source of information. I have seen color photography develop. All these are precious instruments for visual instruction, to say nothing of television and its future. Being faced today with a shortage of time, I think it very important to take all these means into consideration. They are sometimes the equivalent of many, many hours of teaching—which could be economized by these means.

I should also like to say one thing, mainly to those interested in architecture and city planning: today we have lived through what we can call in architecture a revolutionary period which developed around the twenties' and early thirties' in this country. As in all movements of that type, everything had to be swept clean and nobody was supposed to talk anymore about such things as aesthetics, beauty, or history of art and architecture. Techniques and functionalism seemed all-inclusive. Today we have certain experience; we no longer believe that "form necessarily follows function," and since, fortunately (thank God!), it does not always do so, we can quietly reconsider this whole matter and recognize that, although form should not be antifunctional, at the same time, it should be beautiful. Form shouldn't strictly follow function because sometimes function alone won't necessarily result in beautiful forms—and we want to see architecture humanized and beautiful. We are not contented with merely functional buildings that do nothing but fulfill certain material needs. We all recognize today that man has not only material but also spiritual needs, and if a building is really functional, it should fulfill not only the material requirements but also the spiritual needs of man.

The young people coming from the transformed schools all over the country have very little background in architectural history and in what we might call the theory and philosophy of architecture. Those subjects have been dropped from the curricula of architecture, and we believe that, in a completely new way—not following past formulas—they should be reestablished. We would like to see two things in the Graduate School of Design: first, that the students from Harvard College are better prepared in the field of visual arts when they enter the School of Design. They get their mathematics courses, physics, calculus, etc., but they haven't been given proper preparation in the history of the visual arts nor in the fundamentals of design—the type of instruction that could be worked out in workshop courses. These workshop courses existed for some years in the School of Design, as you may all know. There was a certain amount of money to support them, they lasted a certain length of time (as long as the funds lasted). I am trying, as my predecessors tried, to reestablish or continue those courses. The situation is difficult because the school couldn't get the tuition from those courses or any money to pay instructors giving those courses.

Secondly, we want to establish new courses dealing with history, with theory and philosophy of architecture, and with urban design, etc. To establish these courses, we are forced to expand

Alexander Calder and Sert, Harvard University Commencement, 1966.

45 ARCHITECTURE AND THE VISUAL ARTS

our program and need a little help in that field, also. We are not doing too badly in the School of Design: we have more money, we raised the tuition—but we consider we could do even better . . . we are ambitious; we would like to do much better still.

We would like the university to register a greater interest in the visual arts and to do something about this, because that would not only mean that we would get more architects and better architects, and better planners, urban designers, and landscape architects in our schools, but it would also mean that we would get more people to appreciate what we are trying to do.

What we want to do is important, because we are trying to build a better environment for man. That is really the broad aim of the professions of architect, landscape architect, and city planner. We are not only trying to build better buildings. We would like to build a better environment, because we think those buildings cannot be separated from their environment. That environment is tremendously important to all of us—architects and nonarchitects, those people in the university and those outside of the university—because a better environment can help shape better people. So, summarizing, what I would like to say is that we want to get more people and better prepared people from Harvard College; we would like to be able by means of exhibits, photography, etc., to do greater publicity work for the school; we want the Graduate School of Design better known to other people.

We would also like the alumni of Harvard to feel that, regardless of past misunderstandings and difficulties between the school and its alumni, the Graduate School of Design is the same old school that they knew. It has changed because life changes, but there has to be a continuity between the past, the present, and the future; otherwise we could not do any architecture or any city planning at all.

5

NEW YORK
ARCHITECTURE AND THE CITY (1955)

This text, probably for a dean's lecture, was written in Sert's last years as president of CIAM, at around the same time that he was teaching a Harvard GSD urban design studio on Times Square. Through careful visual analysis and reference to specific examples, the essay points the way toward an "architecture that takes the urban possibilities into consideration." Especially notable is Sert's criticism here of the "dream cities of functionalist architecture conceived in the twenties, where high buildings would be surrounded by vast public parks" as "an anti-civic Utopia." At the same time, Sert praises the new pattern set by the United Nations Headquarters (1947–52) and Skidmore, Owings & Merrill's Lever House (1950–52), suggesting that the latter indicates the possibilities of a new urbanism that combines light-filled skyscrapers with lowrise buildings, "making use of patios and gardening."

The text also indicates Sert's support for New York City mayor Robert F. Wagner's efforts to produce a new zoning code. Wagner had been chair of the New York City Planning Commission in 1947, and had commissioned the architecture firm of Harrison, Ballard & Allen to prepare a new zoning ordinance, which was published in 1950 as the Plan for Rezoning the City of New York. After being elected mayor in 1953, Wagner continued his efforts to create a new zoning ordinance, and in 1956, a second architectural firm, Voorhees, Walker, Smith & Smith, was commissioned to draft a new zoning resolution, which became law in 1961.[1] Their predecessor firm, Voorhees Walker, Foley & Smith, whose chief designer was also Ralph Walker, had designed a large, relatively high-density mixed-use housing complex for 35,000 people called Fresh Meadows in Queens in 1946–49, which was admired by Lewis Mumford.[2] Here Sert also praises its "more than suburban" character.

EM

The last ten years have brought great changes in the architectural skin of New York City. These changes, on the surface, are giving the city a "new look."

Until recent years, the design elements of the traditional styles were persistently applied to the new architectural scale imposed by the skyscrapers; and they served, in a way, as units of measure, establishing ties in scale between the past and the present. For example, the double-hung sashes in the highest buildings were of the same size as those of Georgian times. They were scaled to man. At one glance we could tell their size. We could imagine the relationship of this size to that of a person standing behind them.

Other traditional architectural elements applied to the skyscrapers on lower floors or in cornices and penthouses helped us measure those buildings. No matter how arbitrary the application of those elements of past times to the architecture of today, they served a purpose of scaling and helping in establishing a transition. But it is the double-hung windows and the repetition of their type and shape that still gives New York scale and unity.

In commenting on architecture in a city, we often forget the whole and look at single buildings only as something standing alone. This attitude, for which architects are to be most blamed, is the cause of many architectural mistakes. A building in a city, especially a crowded city like New York, does not stand alone. It is part of a physical environment. When architects "sell" a project to a client, they generally represent their building in a rendering or model where the buildings around it, if shown, are greyed out. The spotlight is on the new structure, which is made to stand out independently from its environment, contrary to what will happen when it is built.

Individualism has been the trend of our times and, as a result, architects have made persistent efforts to build, ignoring the environment of buildings, not integrating them to the city as a whole. The results are only too apparent. With the arrival of functionalism, urban design has become a no-man's land: the architect leaving it to the city planner; the city planner, to the architect. Fortunately, things are now moving in the opposite direction, and the last five years have witnessed a growing interest in this field, especially amongst the younger architects, who are increasingly aware of the close ties between buildings and their environment.

In past times, cities developed with certain principles of harmony and measure taken into consideration. The nineteenth century ignored all rules of city growth, and the unprecedented development of the modern metropolis, encouraged by the industrial revolution, broke all those rules and precedents. New York is a product of this explosive growth, but it is also an

Sert with Paul Lester Wiener and staff at the Town Planning Associates' New York office, circa 1955. Courtesy Center for Creative Photography, University of Arizona © 1991 Hans Namuth Estate.

outstanding example of architectural courage. Its architecture taken as a whole impresses us by its strength more than by its beauty. It is an expression of will and decision. Its beauty derives from that expression. The builders of the great New York did nothing timid or small. The hard skyline of Manhattan, especially when seen in that clear diamond light that is so typical of New York, is beautiful in its brutality.

One cannot help admiring the greatness and courage of the designers of old skyscrapers, of the great railroad stations, or of the "El." The bridges and the warehouses, even the repetitious brownstones, had a character and a unity. None of these buildings could be called pretty. They were all uncompromisingly hard and heavy. Such structures as the Brooklyn Bridge, the Grand Central Concourse, or the Lincoln Building are expressions of that character, courage, and beauty which are New York's. It is a difficult task for an architect building in the city today to live up to the New York tradition of courage and greatness. Can our generation match the past ones? It is true that we have more and better building materials and methods than they did. But, as those have expanded and improved, costs have gone up and buildings have become increasingly complicated by new mechanical equipment and controls, and the task of the architect is a harder one today than it ever was.

Architecture is going through revolutionary changes: the greatest since the Gothic cathedrals came to life. But what we have come to call modern or contemporary architecture has not yet found a complete architectural vocabulary. It still is in its early and more primitive shape. The coming generations may consider us barbarians.

Examples of this contemporary architecture—bad, mediocre, and good—have multiplied in the last years throughout the city. They are changing its skin. Good examples are few. Good architecture is always rare, no matter what the style. Modern architecture is no exception. New basic types of modern buildings have developed. They are replacing the old ones, and in every corner we see new office buildings, shops, or apartments of the modern type, the plain brick fronts with large horizontal windows, or the corner window in the new apartments.

The office buildings with alternating strips of glass and brick, known as the "layer cake" types, have no elements of beauty and are no aesthetic improvement in relation to what they have replaced. The shapes of these structures, governed by building and zoning regulations imposing setbacks, ignore proportions and good design, and are not improving the looks of New York's main avenues. The architect can only dress up the ziggurat shapes imposed by outmoded zoning restrictions. The wedding or layer-cake buildings are inevitable results. They are taking over midtown Manhattan. They are the most genuine expression of the latest Manhattan boom. The continuous ribbon windows lack the human scale of those in the older buildings. They give a factory-like appearance to office buildings. The glass modules and opening panels are usually poorly proportioned, combining badly with the brick-faced strips of similar width. The whole has a cheap, utilitarian quality lacking visual interest. Let us hope that this fashion will be discontinued as better formulas make their appearance.

The all-glass façade presents much greater possibilities of variety. In the coming years we may see the use of other materials, such as enamel plates in bright, durable colors, that will combine with glass better than the brick or other heavier material. Aluminum is a step in this direction. There will be an increasing use of factory-made wall units.

SOM, Lever House, New York, 1950–52. Its massing was praised by Sert as a model for future high-density urban development.

The U.N. Secretariat has set a new pattern in the city, which has already been improved by the Lever House building on Park Avenue. This last is possibly the most significant structure in New York, as it may set a new pattern of wide application. The combination of slab skyscrapers with the low buildings can offer a great variety of agreeable solutions. The free-standing slab receiving light from all sides seems to be the right approach to high buildings. The contrast of the slab with the low structures of walk-up scale, making use of patios and gardening, makes good use of land and gives plenty of air around the office slab. This is an architectural solution that could be extended throughout the city if new height-zoning regulations were enacted. In other terms, it is architecture that takes the urban possibilities into consideration. It counts on the environment.

It may pay to be more generous with land in spite of its high cost. Rockefeller Center started a trend in leaving small open spaces—a mall with a flower bed and a skating rink—to make the place more attractive and human. That little open space has attracted people by the millions. Those few flowers and Christmas trees have done more for the center than all its other features. Rockefeller Center is more than a building on the sidewalk. It is a group of buildings related to one another and to some space left open. Lever House adopts a more modern approach and, though smaller in scale, carries this further by raising part of the structure on stilts. The skyscrapers have been unfairly blamed for increasing congestion. This is because they have been placed on the old street fronts in unplanned surroundings. When skyscrapers are integrated in the city and when roads, parking facilities, etc., are designed to take them, no congestion should result. Manhattan House is another rare example of architecture that takes the urban environment into consideration. The placing of the building in the central area of the block and, by this happy idea, leaving space between building and street line makes for needed space, better light, and broader view, and facilitates car accesses. If such a design were repeated across the street, we could have a fairer idea of its possibilities. Better still, of course, if such high blocks could alternate with lower structures and courts every two blocks, this would add to the greenery and spaciousness.

The dream cities of functionalist architecture conceived in the twenties, in which high buildings would be surrounded by vast public parks, would be an anti-civic Utopia. Many architects and city planners are now convinced that such cities developed as continuous parks would lack urban quality and visual interest. We need shops, lights, life near the ground. When in the city, we want to feel these elements around us. The fine new parkways bring the country closer to the city. The city can be beautiful and remain the city in this way. When we leave it, we should move to an entirely different environment.

The more desirable trend in our cities seems to be for them to become more humanized, more congenial to man, more livable and enjoyable. All this can be attained without destroying their economic structure: keeping land values and consequently taxation at a steady level, permitting intense use of land and high densities in certain sectors. The few samples of new patterns in New York City, such as Rockefeller Center, the United Nations, Lever House, Manhattan House, etc., are still only small attempts but prove this to be possible. If the trends in this direction are encouraged by new zoning and building codes (such as those proposed by Harrison, Ballard & Allen in their *Plan for the Rezoning of the City of New York* (1950), these changes in the city could become more than skin deep.

Architecture in the city cannot change in a radical way until the urban pattern is also changed, affecting the whole physical environment. I believe in the coming generation of young Americans, architects, city planners, clients, government officials, etc. Theirs is the task of making these changes possible. They have the faith and the drive.

The large housing developments in New York are, as a whole, gloomy and uninspiring and can in no way compare to the beautiful parkways, the East River and Westside Drive, bridges such as the George Washington and the Whitestone, and some office buildings, such as those previously mentioned. Housing in general (a few developments excepted) consists of monotonous brick blocks, tightly grouped, colorless, and badly landscaped. Some recently built groups already look slummy. As previously stated, existing legislation and bad standards are responsible for these poor results. A modification of these codes and standards is imperative. The quantity of work done in the last ten years is impressive, but the quality lags far behind. One cannot expect people to live happily in such depressing environments. Good architecture cannot always be produced, but more congenial and amiable surroundings, a more human scale, better proportions, greater variety in heights of buildings, a more exciting relationship of open areas, and the introduction of such life-giving elements as bright colors, water, and plants do not seem unattainable.

Changes in codes should permit and encourage the use of light wall units for housing as are already applied in offices. These prefabricated elements would give a lighter, more agreeable look to apartment buildings and could open a broad new field to industry. The heavy brick walls that only carry their own weight, used as an enclosure of a high skeleton structure, are outmoded and senseless. A modification of the building code permitting the use of light, fireproof prefabricated units is badly needed. A careful analysis and study of the possibilities of prefabrication applied to high apartment buildings should be made. Prefabrication seems to have a wider application in the field of apartment blocks than in that of detached one-family houses, as apartment dwellers do not generally have definite ideas about the outside looks of their homes, as they do when a one-family house is called for.

The last ten years, since the end of World War II, have also witnessed a great suburban growth. Better designed homes with larger windows, and a few better planned developments, can be seen around the city. They would require more space for comment, but we are here dealing with the more urban or civic architecture—that in areas closer to the heart of the city.

Developments such as Fresh Meadows, for example, are more than suburban in character. They present many good points, such as shopping and parking facilities, use of walk-ups and high blocks for contrast and variety, and better landscaping, etc. They are more humane and livable than the larger housing complexes built in central areas, where no effort to develop a more pleasing environment seems to have been attempted.

The midtown bus terminal is an interesting building because it shows an example of integration of architecture and road engineering. Consequently, it is a structure related to the city and conceived as part of it. To date, road and bridge engineering is far ahead of architecture in the city.

Voorhees, Walker, Foley & Smith, Fresh Meadows, Queens, New York, 1949. Thomas Airviews, New York Life Archives.

One of the greatest changes in the looks of the city is the variety of modern shops, stores, and restaurants; partly the work of architects, decorators, and display experts. There has been tremendous progress in this field in every large city, but it is possibly in New York where these innovations are greatest and where display techniques have reached a peak.

When dealing with architecture in a city, we forget the important role played by billboards, neon lettering, signs of all kinds, and advertising in general. This is especially important in spots like Times Square, where those elements are part of the architecture and give a character to the place. The grey façades behind the billboards, work of the architect, are dead and forgotten. The modern architect working in an urban environment will have to plan for those changeable mobile elements, his architecture being partly a container for such elements. If modern design techniques were applied to Times Square as a whole, and the best modern artists allowed to participate, New York could have the most magnificent stage set ever conceived.

What further changes can we expect in the near future? It is worth our while to consider the latest trends in New York architecture and try to imagine how these ways of building are going to change the city tomorrow—not only its looks, but its structure.

I am not a believer in decentralization as a remedy to all evils, and I think that high densities are compatible with a good way of living. But high densities require careful comprehensive planning, and New York has reached a phase where only careful planning can solve its problems. The existing trends are toward a continued intense land use, more high buildings usually replacing lower ones. There is also a new scattering of office buildings in midtown Manhattan. Park Avenue from the East Thirties to the Sixties is rapidly changing its character from a residential street to an office and business area. Sixth Avenue is not developing as it should. The new buildings, or the great majority of them, have not taken into consideration the need for light and air. Buildings today continue to pile up, regardless of the critical conditions that lack of air and light will bring to the city. Only their fronts have changed in looks; they are modern on the surface; inside, only the new materials and equipment make them modern. Their plans are still governed by outmoded codes.

The old street system remains unclassified and unbroken. There has been no serious attempt at separation of traffic and pedestrians in different streets. In this respect, New York may soon remain behind some smaller cities that are considering new classified street patterns for their downtown districts. The center of New York faces increasing traffic congestion. After establishing one-way avenues and limiting parking time along them, the next measures will have to be more radical in character. Surgery will have to intervene, the parking problem will have to be faced in all its scope and complexity, and means of keeping many private cars out of the midtown and downtown areas may be one possible solution. This would imply large parking spaces or parking garages at the periphery, well connected with the rapid transit systems. Commuters could largely benefit by saving time if such systems are established. New car models designed for use in the city may be another answer. The ratio of parking space is about six to ten, if we compare small European cars to the average American types. Statistics prove that the average private car transports only about $1\,^2/_3$ people into the city. Car designers do not seem to consider the high cost of land and scarcity of space in the cities. This is another field in which coordination of design is imperative.

I believe that the great majority of New Yorkers would like their city to become more livable and human. New York can keep its greatness, but it is no longer a fast-growing child. It has reached maturity, an age that demands certain responsibilities. And as a world capital, New York has to face them, replacing unplanned growth by balanced, planned development.

The city has to change more than its skin or its face. It has to change its structure to adapt itself to the requirements of modern living; to benefit by modern building techniques, to make full use of modern materials in its buildings; all geared to make life better and more agreeable, to attract more people, more and better business. Its new face cannot be designed by the architect alone. All powers governing the growth of the city have to partake in this task. New and better plans will come out of this joint endeavor. With new codes and regulations that will take modern city planning principles as their basis, the architectural revolution could then reach its full development. It will no longer be a face-lifting operation. It will come out of the new roots. The changes we have seen in the last ten years are only a modest preview of the future.

6

CIAM X
DUBROVNIK (1956)

This event, originally planned for then-French-controlled Algiers and organized by a group of CIAM youth members called Group X, was the last full CIAM conference.[1] Sert's opening and closing remarks in Dubrovnik are his last contributions to the organization, in which he had played a key role since the late 1930s and of which he had been president since 1947.

Sert's opening talk emphasizes that the purpose of this event, as was also the case at CIAM 9 in 1953, was to reach enough agreement among the architects present to create a "Charter of Habitat." This would replace the earlier CIAM Athens Charter and would provide design and planning direction for the vast urbanization processes then beginning around the world. The effort was fraught with difficulties: CIAM was already divided in the postwar years between strict functionalists like the Dutch architect Willem van Tijen, who saw no need to modify the prewar modernist approaches now often associated with Hannes Meyer, and the more urban and arts-oriented directions advocated in different ways by Le Corbusier, Sert, Aldo van Eyck, and the Italian CIAM group, led by Ernesto Rogers of the firm BBPR. In this already conflicted context, Team 10 began to question both the prewar CIAM focus on the four functional planning categories of work, housing, leisure, and recreation, as well as Sert's and Rogers's new emphasis on the heart of the city.

The result was an inability for CIAM to continue to work collaboratively, as Team 10 members Van Eyck, Jacob Bakema, Alison and Peter Smithson, Georges Candilis, and others insisted on questioning all the terminology and organizational aspects of CIAM. The "middle generation" of CIAM that Team 10 revolted against were President Sert; Sigfried Giedion, the secretary-general; and MARS member Jaqueline Tyrwhitt, assisted in Dubrovnik by the Zagreb architect Drago Ibler and the Swiss CIAM member Alfred Roth. This Team 10 revolt against his own admirers was tacitly supported by Le Corbusier, who chose not to attend CIAM 10.

In this opening text from that event, Sert outlines the major turning points in the history of CIAM and announces that it now seems to be time for a new generation to take over the organization.

At the end of CIAM 10, on August 11, 1956, Sert delivered his last public speech to the group. Recognizing the expansion of modern architecture in many parts of the world, Sert called here for a new CIAM structure organized by continents, since it was becoming difficult for many of the members to travel to Europe for the congesses, held every two years. Sert emphasized that the central problem for the organization remained the need to provide modern ways of thinking about the provision of shelter in the fast-growing cities of the world. He also suggested the continuation of the organization's activities in various locations worldwide by naming various members practicing in Tokyo, Oslo, Warsaw, Vienna, Geneva, Zagreb, Haifa, and Bogotá, and teaching at institutions such as the University of Waseda, the TU Delft, the ETH Zurich, Milan Polytechnic, Cambridge University, the Architectural Association, IIT, the University of Illinois, and the University of Pennsylvania, as well as at Harvard.

Sert's efforts to continue CIAM on this new world basis, directed by a new Council of younger members that included Peter Smithson, Bakema, and Roth, did not succeed. At the next CIAM meeting, organized by Team 10 and held in Otterlo, the Netherlands, and called CIAM '59, it was decided to cease using the CIAM name.

EM

OPENING COMMENTS

We are now opening the tenth Congress of CIAM, and I want to greet the delegates and friends here present. I know that it has not been easy for many of them to get here, but I hope that our stimulating work and the pleasure of meeting in such a beautiful city will compensate any sacrifice. I want to thank the organizers of the Congress for their help. We are all aware that it is not easy to organize such a Congress during the summer season when such places as this one are crowded and transportation is difficult to obtain, but I am sure that this tenth Congress will represent a turning point in the history of CIAM.

We are going to deal with the future structure of the human habitat, a rather ambitious subject which we have been studying and debating in previous meetings; with other names, this same object has been our constant concern for many years. After the Brussels meeting of 1930, CIAM realized that the individual buildings or small groups of buildings could not be properly studied if considered out of the general complex of the community. This led CIAM to the analysis of the city as a whole and the formulation of the Athens Charter of 1933. This

Definitions of "Habitat," from CIAM 10 Dubrovnik 1956 (gta archives, ETH Zurich: CIAM archives, courtesy of Laurent Stalder). Both CIAM 9 and CIAM 10 were intended to produce a Charter of Habitat to supersede the CIAM Athens Charter.

```
                                                          53
B. THE HABITAT

What means HABITAT?

"HABITAT":    Terme de Botanique, lieu spécialement habité
              par une espèce végétale, on l'applique aussi
              aux animaux et à l'homme. L'habitat le mieux
              approprié à leurs aptitudes natives et à leurs
              besoins futurs.
                         Dictionnaire de la langue francaise,
                         Paris 1882, Vol. III, p. 1967.

"HABITAT":    The locality in which an animal naturally grows
              and lives.
                         Oxford Dictionary, Vol.V.

"HABITAT":    As Gropius writes us, you will find a similar
              explanation for the same term in Webster's
              American Dictionary.

"HABITAT":    "L' Habitat" représente les conditions de vie
              dans le milieu total (implique par conséquent
              les grandes modifications qui s'annoncent sur
              l'occupation du territoire par le travail de
              l'homme de la civilisation machiniste. C'est
              l'état de confusion et de déchirement actuel).
                         Le Corbusier à Emery, le 9 mai 1955.

All these "definitions" are concerned with an atmosphere
properous to "grow and live". To create this atmosphere
for the human being is the principle aim of CIAM.
```

is a document of urbanism, it is a "charter of urbanism," but it stated that the city has to be considered a part of a larger complex or region defined by geographic, political, social, and economic factors.

The following Congress, that of Paris in 1937, dealt with dwelling and recreation and limited its studies to residential sectors. It explored the relationship of the different types of dwellings to land ownership and to open areas and, briefly, to community services. The community core was not considered in the way we do now, but this Congress carried on from the Athens Charter in trying to develop its governing principles as applied to residential areas. The idea then was to develop the Athens Charter in each of its fundamental chapters. The Congress was aware then that the Athens Charter should be completed in successive Congresses. Before CIAM could meet again, the war started. Our next meeting was one of reunion at Bridgwater in 1947 after the war. Ten years had gone by since the last meeting, and the Congress felt that the aim of CIAM should be restated, and it was thus formulated: "To work for the creation of a physical environment that will satisfy man's emotional and material needs and stimulate his spiritual growth." The force behind CIAM that has brought us together during the last twenty-eight years has been a common belief and a confidence in the destiny of man, in human dignity, a faith in a better future, in man's capacity to build a better world. An awareness of the great possibilities of modern technical knowledge and recent scientific discoveries to make that better world a reality if put to a constructive use. Immediate, not remote, possibilities to build better cities with homes, working and meeting places designed to man's measure, to serve his needs both spiritual and physical, to make our lives worth living as stated in our aims in Bridgwater.

The Bergamo Congress concerned itself with a means of expressing our problems and suggested solutions in a new graphic way. Le Corbusier's Grille [CIAM Grid] system was tested and enthusiastically accepted. This graphic expression permitted comparisons and easier understanding of essential factors and gave us a more direct means of communication with the outside world. In their structure, the Grilles follow the classification in four functions of the Athens Charter. They are a continuation of research in the same direction, following the constant CIAM line.

Hoddesdon in 1951 followed Bergamo, and the subject chosen was the Core of the City. This also tended to complete the Athens Charter, breaking the too rigid and elementary barriers established in that document with its division of all urban life into four functions. The accent on interrelationships of functions was already in the core. The results of this Congress were very important and their influence considerable. A new and basic chapter was added to the Athens Charter.

Aix-en-Provence in 1953 was to deal with the total concept of the habitat as it refers to residential areas. The subject was large and difficult. The material presented in graphic form was very good. The people were too many for a working Congress and the time to meet too short. As a result, no resolutions or final statements could be worked out, but Aix was a very important step to what came afterward. It made CIAM groups more interested in the habitat theme, as documents shown made clearer the shortcomings of the Athens Charter. After long debates a new approach to the subject of the habitat was apparent.

An emphasis on human relation, the constructive work done in the last La Sarraz meeting, is proof that CIAM is over the difficulties and hesitations and has found a new line that is a continuation of the old. The Grilles prepared under the guidance of Group X, responsible for the technical organization of the Congress, are remarkable documents proving that CIAM is always a working Congress exploring new ground, searching new approaches, and finding new directives.

These will influence in the future, as they have done in the past, work now carried out around the world by younger people, especially by students in every country. We can say this *now that so many barriers have disappeared and modern architecture and planning principles are being accepted around the world.* We hope that the meeting of minds and identity of aims that brought CIAM to life twenty-eight years ago will continue to give positive results. These are expected from us by the students of architecture and city planning in the major universities, and we cannot let them down when so much is expected of us. Korsmo has suggested that CIAM establish some organization of university groups that could exchange ideas and work on problems along the lines now being determined by the Congress.[2] This seems a happy idea, as it is among the younger people that our Congress has a greater following.

But CIAM is now faced with changes—the inevitable changes determined by the inescapable cycle of life that requires a constant renewal. *The Congress is twenty-eight years old, and twenty-five years represent a new generation.* CIAM is still a young Congress. Our heated debates are a proof of this, and our members can be classified only as young, younger, and youngest—but the young ones are very busy, and new blood is needed in all living organisms. CIAM is not like other Congresses; it is a living organism and demands work and energy, and the youngest can do this task better than those who have been here for twenty-five years. We regret the absence in this Congress of Le Corbusier, Walter Gropius, Helena Syrkus, and Cornelis van Eesteren. They all have sent kind messages that will be read to you, but we should prefer their presence to their letters, as CIAM cannot be guided by remote control. In agreement with our statutes we should elect a new council.

It is time for a change in the Congress direction within the framework of continuity of the general aims that make CIAM remain what it is, a Congress different from all others. We should not forget that these differences are our force. By taking a critical attitude toward our own work and by becoming a working Congress, CIAM has opened new subjects to discussion. *It is today the smallest, poorest, but most stimulating group organization in the architectural field.*

Changes may bring us a different CIAM, a new CIAM, but this is natural and healthy. I am sure that we all will like to remain in some capacity active in CIAM, as our Congress is an active Congress, one of participants. It is up to CIRPAC to determine what this capacity should be. Those of us who have been here for many years may represent a factor of continuity, and if this is the desire of this Congress I am sure that none of us will be unwilling to help, within the limits of time at our disposal. *The old should be replaced by the better, not only by the new. It is useful to review our views and methods with the objective of obtaining clearer views and developing better methods.* A diversity of trends exists today in our midst, and many "certainties" of the twenties and thirties appear questionable. It is only natural that CIAM should register

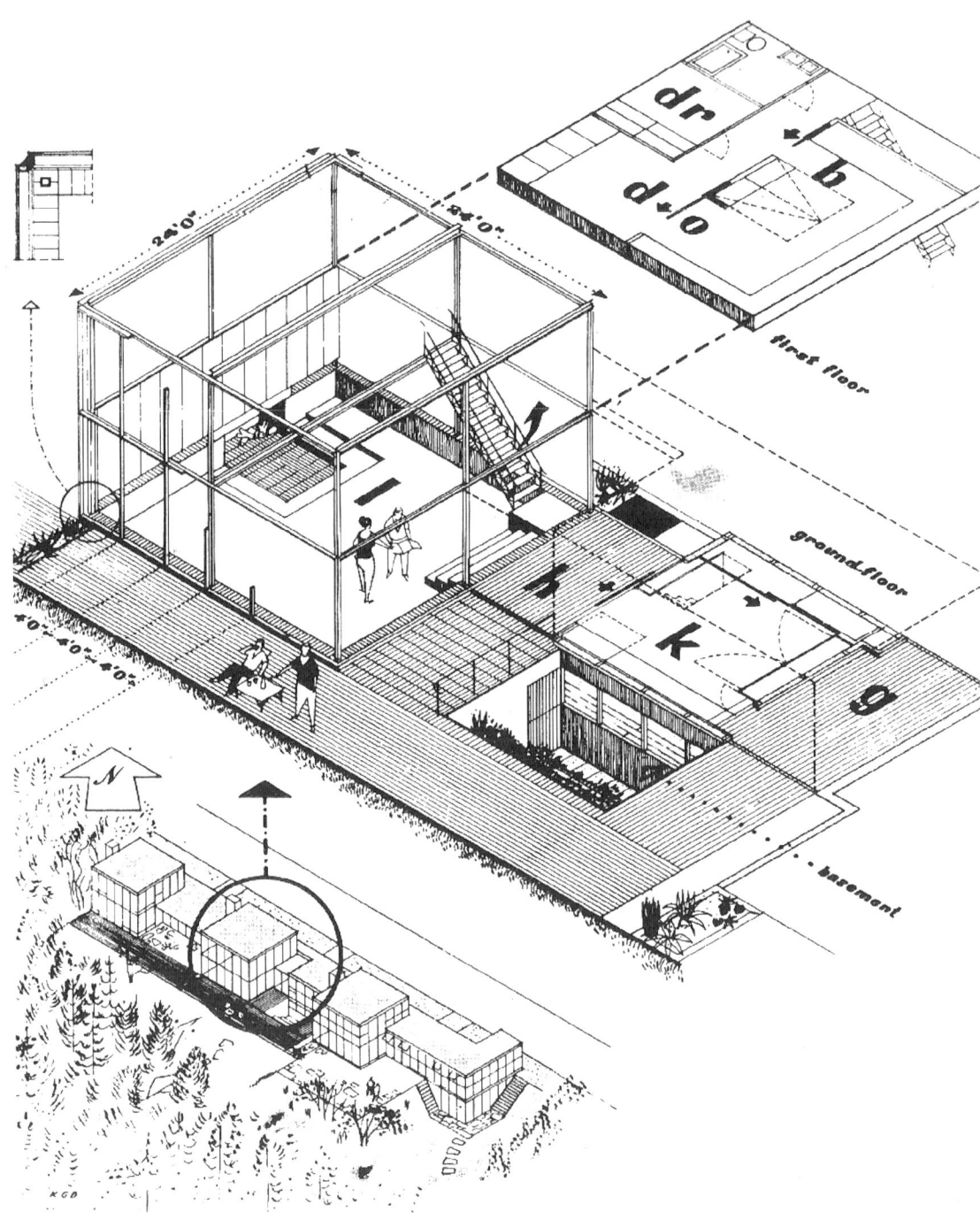

Arne Korsmo with Grete Prytz Kittelsen, House, Planetveien, Oslo, 1956. From Christian Norberg-Schulz, *The Functionalist Arne Korsmo* (Oslo: Universitetsforlaget, 1986), 104. Korsmo was appointed by Sigfried Giedion, the CIAM secretary-general, as the Norwegian CIAM representative in 1950, where he led the PAGON group in Oslo.

these differences. This is a proof that our organization is not an academic organization tied to a doctrine but that it's alive, and "live" is mutation. These differences are CIAM. This structure should be kept in the future, and CIAM, no matter how small and poor, *should continue to be an independent organization.* In this lies the future of our Congress.

Many of our members have worked very hard for the Congress since our last meeting, preparing Grilles, formulating documents, translating texts, etc. Group X was entrusted by the Council and the CIRPAC with the formulation of the program for CIAM X and the organization of the material to be presented. This group has done an outstanding job. Previously, the North African group did considerable work in the organization of the Algiers Congress, which had to be abandoned because of conditions there. Later, Alfred Roth and Drago Ibler were charged with the organization of this tenth Congress. The program formulated by CIAM X and agreed to by the council and the CIRPAC will be read by Jaqueline Tyrwhitt right away. After this, our work will start; let us roll up our sleeves. The task is not an easy one.

CLOSING COMMENTS

We are going to deal today with the future of CIAM. It may be the last time that I address you as president of this association, and I would like to say a few words on that subject before we get into the actual details. I do not know how many of you are aware that CIAM has grown much larger in the last years. This doesn't refer to the actual membership of CIAM, which is about the same as it has been, but there are many more people who know about CIAM and there are many more people interested in what CIAM is doing. I can feel this in my classes at Harvard University, where I get young people coming from every part of the world: Asia, North and South Africa, Europe, South America, etc. From the moment they come, I realize that they know about CIAM and are interested in CIAM. It has been our duty and our responsibility to try to live up to the expectations of all these young people. And it is going to be your duty and your responsibility—those who now take over—to live up to the expectations people have about what CIAM is doing and how CIAM can give direction to their work.

I believe, after these years of experience, that the international—or intercontinental—character of CIAM should be stressed. We cannot ignore the great problems of the world today. It is all right and good that certain experiments and certain particular lines of interest, such as we are dealing with now, are carried on. The present one is a broad topic, but it has been handled mainly on the basis of small examples. I have looked at the Grids. They are very interesting, there is excellent material, but the exhibition is not very broad and it has, to my way of seeing, one main defect: it is too much restricted to one area of the world. It could all be fitted into a few very small corners of the world, and—as is natural, of course—the Grids occupy themselves mainly with the problems of that corner of the world. This doesn't mean that CIAM has not got groups in other parts of the world, and it is disappointing that many of the more remote groups do not come often to CIAM and have not been participating very actively. It is important, though, that these groups have greater participation, and something should be done in the new structure of CIAM to facilitate this.

You must realize, of course, that it's all very well to say, for example: "But we cannot go to America—the trip is too expensive." But the trip is also expensive for the people on the other side. This was more unbalanced right after the war because of the different conditions in Europe and America. But these conditions are no longer so unbalanced now. And I believe that other countries—and I don't say only America, in the future it will be also Japan, perhaps India and other places in the world—will want to have their own CIAM meetings, and the new organization should provide for this. Some kind of federal structure should be given to CIAM so that there can be CIAM meetings without all of us having to come together.

I will give you a precise case in which such things could work very well. There is a Pan-American Congress of Architects that takes place every two or three years. This is, like all large Congresses, a grouping of architects without any kind of discrimination as to their attitudes or ideas. Everybody who wants to go and can pay for the trip, or have the trip paid for him, goes to this Congress. But what happens is that many young people can go to these Congresses because their government pays or because they can pay themselves as the journey is shorter than a trip to Europe. The same may be true of Japan. I have been working with many Japanese architects. They are a very brilliant crowd, and I believe that in Japan there is going to be a very important development of modern architecture and planning in the coming years. They should have an opportunity of meeting with the countries closer to them in a CIAM meeting, even if a number in this part of the world cannot attend. It would be narrow-minded of us, I think, to try to restrict CIAM activities to Western Europe. That was all right in the twenties and early thirties but is no good now. We have seen the expansion of modern architecture to all parts of the world, and in some of them with remarkable results. What has been done, for example, in Brazil is certainly outstanding, and I believe, as I was telling you, that Japan will follow.

Another thing that I wanted to tell you is that though the subjects that CIAM has been working on are very interesting, we cannot remain detached from the main world problems. We have to broaden our horizons. Many of us may feel an inclination to tackle certain specific problems. I think we should all work individually on the problems we like. But as a Congress as a whole we cannot ignore that there is a tremendous problem of shelter today. Millions of people urgently need the application of modern ways of thinking and of approaching these problems, the application of modern techniques to their limited and sometimes very restricted local conditions, new use of their own materials; a series of directives that they haven't got. And this precisely occurs in the parts of the world that have new potentialities and in the cities that are growing faster. Our old European cities have ceased their great periods of growth. It is in the places where the world is expanding at this terrific tempo—much faster than anything we see around us here—that help is most critically needed. And I think that CIAM cannot stand aside from these problems, no matter how interesting other investigations may be.

Up to now CIAM has produced several ways of expanding its ideas. We have mainly done this by our Congresses themselves and the people who come to them; but also by our publications and by talks, teaching, and contacts with people in government and others, and by television, a medium that lends itself excellently to the expression of our ideas. I think all these means should be increased. CIAM has to continue publishing books and articles and giving people pictures of what we are doing in traveling exhibits and other ways. But besides

BBPR, Corso Francia apartments, Turin, Italy, 1957. Designed by CIAM Council member and 1954 Harvard GSD visitor Ernesto Rogers, whose ideas about the importance of urban context for modern architecture inspired many architects in later decades.

Germán Samper (Esguerra, Sáenz, Urdaneta, Samper), Biblioteca Luis Ángel Arango, Bogotá, 1958-64. After early CIAM involvement, Samper went on to become a major architect in Colombia.

all this I think we have another medium that we cannot neglect, because we are strategically placed to use it, and it is one where we have our greatest source for the future. This medium is in architectural and planning education. I do not know how many of you realize how many of us are now giving a great part of our time to teaching. This morning I made a list.

First there's our friend Korsmo from Norway, who reminded me about the need for doing something about this. Then there are Giuseppe Samonà, Piero Bottoni, Ernesto Rogers, Lodovico Belgiojoso and others in Italy (we have a special CIAM Summer School in Venice thanks to the efforts of the Italian Group).

In the more remote countries we have several extremely good young architects, like Germán Samper, who is working and teaching in Bogotá. We have, of course, people like Sigfried Giedion, who has for many years been teaching in Zurich and elsewhere, and now we have Leslie Martin in England, who has been charged with the organization, or reorganization, of a school of architecture in Cambridge University. We have Arieh Neumann in Haifa; Mies van der Rohe in Chicago; the Syrkuses and Jerzy Soltan in Warsaw; Van Eesteren and Van der Broek in Holland; Blanche Lemco in Philadelphia [later Blanche van Ginkel in Toronto];

Drago Ibler, Wooden Tower, Zagreb, Croatia, 1956 (Croatian Society of Architects, courtesy of Ivan Rupnik). Ibler was a postwar leader of CIAM in the former Yugoslavia, and he organized CIAM 10 in Dubrovnik with Jaqueline Tyrwhitt.

Peter Smithson in London; Wilhelm Schuette in Vienna; Georges Brera in Geneva; Gabriel Guévrékian in Illinois; Drago Ibler in Zagreb; and Yoshizaka Takamasa at the University of Waseda, which happens to be one of the best architectural schools in the world at the moment—they got two successive prizes at the Brazil Biennale. I, myself, with several others here, am working at Harvard University.

So you see, we really have a tremendous network of people teaching in all these architectural schools, and I think a great benefit both for the students and for ourselves in CIAM can be derived by establishing closer contacts between us. We can perhaps sometimes try to help students who wish to go from one school to another by giving them a recommendation from friend to friend. We know the people who go through our classes much better than from casual acquaintance at a Congress; when they have been working in our classes we have had an opportunity to judge them and to measure their qualities. By increasing our contacts we could perhaps suggest people as possible future members of CIAM, as well as gain much ourselves from the exchange of ideas and plans. I won't go so far as to say we can perhaps exchange professors; maybe that can come one day, but it's a more difficult affair. Anyway, I do think that some kind of contact between the people who are in the teaching field and are at the same time members of CIAM would be most useful.

I do not want to be long, but I would just like to remind you that all things in the world today build toward action. Action is demanded of us. It is all very well to debate all these interesting subjects that we have been talking about for the last twenty-five years, but it would be a total failure if we continue debating endlessly. I don't mean by that that debates should in any way be curtailed. There can be no established doctrine. This must change and evolve as the times change and evolve and as people and the world situation changes. But I do believe that all the energies of CIAM should not be devoted to these debates, no matter how interesting. I believe that CIAM should have groups of members directly concerned with action and how to get the ideas of CIAM into the circles of government; how to get the ideas of CIAM to become reality. Gropius was insistent in his letter and in talks I have had with him on this point. The young people coming into CIAM are going to ask not only "What do you think about these things?" but "How are you going to do them?" A lot has been said in CIAM but, in comparison with the speeches we have made, the books we have written, the exhibitions we have prepared, very little has actually been done. I would like the people who are now coming into the Congresses to be conscious of the little that has been done in proportion to the lot that has been said. With that in mind I think you will be able to do an excellent job—and go to it!

7
HARVARD
URBAN PROBLEM AND OPPORTUNITY (1957)

This article was published in *Harvard Today*, a now defunct alumni magazine, just as Sert was creating the Harvard University Office of the Planning Coordinator with the young recent GSD graduate Harold Goyette and others. Harvard, like Yale, had begun to expand greatly in the postwar years as federal research money poured in during the Cold War, and Sert was appointed to the Cambridge Planning Board at this time. He recognized that the existing Harvard campus pattern of neo-Georgian quadrangles with a few lowrise modern buildings, adjacent to busy commercial streets, would not be able to accommodate the institution's growing need for more parking and for more instructional and research spaces. He then initiated the process of planning the future of the campus so that large new additions to it would fit within its dense and historic context without overwhelming its historic surroundings. His campus interventions, such as Holyoke Center, Peabody Terrace student housing, and eventually the Harvard Science Center demonstrate the built outcomes of these ideas. In addition to the model of the Cambridge University campus in England, Sert also mentions here the new Temple University campus in Philadelphia, then being planned by Willo von Moltke and others. Sert appointed Von Moltke director of the Harvard Urban Design Program in 1964. Sert was identified for this article as a "special consultant to the University in problems of planning, development, and design, as well as president of CIAM and an internationally known architect and master planner." His plans for Lima, Medellín, Cali, Bogotá (with Le Corbusier), and "two new communities in the Orinoco Valley (Venezuela) for U.S. Steel" were noted, along with his consulting work for the Venezuelan Ministry of Public Works and the National Planning Office of the Cuban government. For the latter it was noted that his current work in Cuba included the Havana Master Plan and "the new Presidential Palace in that city." Though not mentioned, all of this work was done with Paul Lester Wiener in the firm Town Planning Associates, New York.

EM

Our universities are growing universities in a growing country. But, as this country grows not only in numbers but in wealth, it is improving its living standards; and this means greater opportunities for many people.

While some university campuses are in the midst of semi-rural or suburban areas and have plenty of open land on their fringes, others, like Harvard University, are in an urban environment with no open, unbuilt land in their immediate neighborhood. Harvard is an urban campus and has the advantages and disadvantages of being part of a city.

It is a part of the City of Cambridge, which happens to be right in metropolitan Boston. The university occupies 142 acres within the City of Cambridge and an additional 133 acres in Boston (only the Soldiers' Field section). Cambridge is one element in the metropolitan constellation, and because of its proximity to the central city or core, it is one of the more developed elements. Cambridge contains very little unbuilt land (10 percent); it has developed up to the city limits.

Harvard is not only an urban campus, but it is a campus in a congested city. Congestion sometimes comes from lack of land and high densities of population, but it is often the result of the misuse of land and lack of planning and foresight. Land, like many other commodities, is frequently wasted. This is not very damaging when there is plenty of it, but it can make life difficult when there is scarcity.

Under such conditions the need for planning becomes more evident. Planning, like traffic controls, may seem unnecessary when there is plenty of space to move in; but it becomes a "must" as congestion grows and interests collide.

It is better to plan ahead of time; to foresee and avoid difficulties is less costly than to correct them. But unfortunately, preventive planning, like preventive medicine, is the exception and not the rule.

As of today, conditions in the City of Cambridge have deteriorated far enough for many people to see that some planning is urgently needed. To improve these conditions and cope with the more pressing problems, a Citizens' Advisory Committee, in which the universities are represented, was formed in June of 1956. President Pusey is a member of this committee. Closer contacts have been established between the Cambridge Planning Board and the university. A pilot plan for Cambridge is under way.

The university, aware of the need to correlate all planning efforts, has organized the Office of the Planning Coordinator. This office will assist in every possible way with the plans for development of the university. It will also contribute to the establishment of effective relation-

View of Harvard Square from Massachusetts Avenue looking south from the Cambridge Common. In 1957, Sert wrote, "Harvard has grown tremendously since 1636, and so has the Cambridge that surrounds the College. Compare the above photo of the Square in 1957 [not shown] with the Burgis-Price view of Harvard in 1743. Like Cambridge University, the Yard is an island of peace protected by the academic buildings that screen it from the traffic and confusion that surrounds it. Harvard intends to keep it that way."

ships between the university and the City of Cambridge, so that Harvard may fulfill its obligation as a responsible element in the community.

Many Harvard planning problems cannot be solved without this coordination of the efforts of the city and the university, and the action or inaction of the city in matters of planning will influence the shape of the future Harvard. Whatever is done in Cambridge to ease the traffic congestion, whatever provisions are taken to provide more parking facilities, and the early undertaking of large-scale renewal and rehabilitation projects are all of vital concern to Harvard.

The university has much to gain if it develops in a planned city. It cannot very well continue to prosper in the midst of growing congestion and blight, no matter how many improvements are made within the campus itself. Harvard has grown and will continue to grow with Cambridge. It is located in the heart of the city, right in the waistline of the butterfly-shaped area defined by the city limits, where roads converge toward Harvard Square. The problems of the City of Cambridge are those of the majority of cities of similar size (100,000 population), but they are aggravated by the proximity of Boston and surrounding developed areas.

The traffic congestion is increased by the great number of automobiles used by students (one car to every 2.7 students) and university staff, many of whom must commute by automobile from points outside the city limits. This is one of the many problems that the university and the city must solve jointly.

A special study to improve parking facilities was undertaken by Harvard recently, but it shows that nothing really efficient can be done unless such a study is part of an overall plan. The Harvard solution to parking will be partly affected by the Cambridge solution, and it will greatly depend on the policy adopted for the Cambridge plan and the new highway system of metropolitan Boston, such as the location of the new Belt Route. The Belt Route is a peripheral highway linking the main roads converging toward the center of Boston. One section of this Belt Route will bisect the City of Cambridge. Other parts of this metropolitan highway system, though not passing through Cambridge, will also influence the flow of traffic inside the city limits.

Traffic congestion in Harvard Square may decrease considerably when the new through highways are built. On the other hand, more commerce and larger office buildings will attract more people to this sector.

It is evident that there is no easy or cheap solution to the parking problem, but the campus, like the city, will have to find some answers and adopt some measures for improvement, otherwise, aggravated conditions will continue.

Will these improvements result from the establishment of large parking lots on the fringes of the campus or beyond? Are multilevel parking lots economically feasible? Or will the answer be to restrict cars, so that only small cars, or no cars at all, are permitted within a certain radius of the campus? Anyhow, it is evident that whenever a building calls for a certain parking area, it should provide for it and not depend on the neighboring streets. Every extension of the campus should be designed with provisions for such needs. Improvised parking lots are encroaching on landscaped areas, and this should be avoided by more careful planning and consolidation of parking lots at certain points so as to leave the more important quadrangles entirely free from traffic.

Holden Chapel in Harvard Yard, 1742. Sert wrote, "Harvard would not be the same without Holden Chapel. Historic monuments like Holden need not be so large as the University of Virginia Rotunda, nor need they be of any fixed design. When Holden was built, Harvard was not building a monument for 1957. Holden was built to fill a need, and its history over the years has shown this. But it has become one of Harvard's most treasured buildings. Only time can determine whether what Harvard builds in this generation [like the Graduate Center, page 75] will become monuments of the future."

A university such as Harvard must keep and improve its green spaces. An urban campus is a cultural center within a city and should set an example of good planning and good design for the city. It is, in a way, a micro city, and its urbanity is the expression of a better, more civilized way of life.

This better way of living cannot be conceived without lawns and trees in properly landscaped, dignified open spaces. This is the only proper natural setting for educational buildings. The quadrangles of today had their ancestors in those of the Greek gymnasiums and the monastic convent cloisters—places for meditation and conversation—where man could find the natural elements, such as trees, plants, and water, congenial to him. All these are elements that our cities have destroyed and not replaced.... Planning that is concerned with the shaping of spaces considers open space as important as covered space inside buildings.

The planner, the architect, and the landscape architect should work hand-in-hand to produce a better balanced and more beautiful physical environment.

But a campus in a congested city has no easy way to expand. It cannot spread much because of lack of open land; and because it can only acquire more land at high cost, it has to make the best possible use of land, and growth in height is one of the answers to this more intense land use.

To expand, the university can do three things:
a) Make better use of the land it has by establishing a more compact plan.
b) Acquire more land, on the fringes of the campus or beyond.
c) Grow in height, and use land more intensely.

There are great possibilities of interior growth by making better use of existing buildings. Interior space can be more efficiently used by remodeling many of the older buildings. Some of these were designed in a wasteful way, as space then was not as costly as it is today; and the whole approach to its use or misuse was different. Many of these buildings have been put to new uses for which they are not well suited. There is a new approach to the use of interior space today that determines the shape, size, and furnishing of rooms, and there are efficiency experts in matters of space allocation.

The acquisition of new land implies a careful study, not only of prices, taxation, and location of parcels, but also of the size and shape of those parcels in terms of their future use. The programming of needs of new buildings and a rough calculation of size and type can be of great help in an intelligent policy for Harvard's future purchases.

The growth in height should take place only where such height will not disturb the view, light, or privacy, or spoil the unity of scale of existing groups of buildings. High buildings require open spaces and carefully planned accesses. If well located, high buildings may solve many problems and permit a more intense use of the land without disturbing the lower buildings around them. Some fringe areas and those along the Charles River may be the best suited for high structures. These should not invade the older quadrangles.

The micro city that is the campus should aim at being a model city, an example of a desirable physical environment. This Harvard is, in more than one way. But the growth of the

Walter Gropius and the Architects Collaborative (TAC), Harvard Graduate Center, 1948.

campus in the conditions of today presents many difficulties and risks the loss of some of the best features.

A good physical environment should provide a balance between open landscaped spaces and built-up areas. It should provide a dignified, well-scaled architecture that is an expression of our times but still can live side by side with buildings of the past. This architecture should be true to our needs, that is, functional, serving its purpose; but human needs are not only material needs. They also are spiritual, and these, too, should be satisfied. This means that architecture everywhere, but especially on a campus, should be more than functional in the actual materialistic interpretation given to this word, meaning only utilitarian.

Such architecture need not always express function or "follow function" literally in its forms, though it should not be antifunctional. It should make adequate use of good materials, old and new, without prejudice. It should be dignified, serene, and harmonious.

The new buildings in the campus should not be simply an imitation of historic styles, because the past cannot be reenacted in architecture, any more than it can in any other field of art or science. The styles of the past, functional in their own time, do not meet our needs today, and they deprive us of the proper use of many modern advantages.

Old buildings made use of space that would be considered wasteful today. Modern buildings, making use of steel or concrete for structures and light materials for nonbearing parts, are by nature more flexible and open; and to superimpose a period façade on such modern structures is wasteful and senseless. A contemporary architecture, expressive of our needs and employing the technical knowledge of our time, is the most appropriate to the cultural center that is a university campus.

Historical development of Cambridge, Massachusetts: map series used by Sert (*Harvard Today*, November 1957, 8). Sert wrote, "In the beginning the Square was little but a crossing of dirt roads and country lanes. In nearby fields cows grazed on the edge of the wilderness which bordered the Yard. As Harvard gradually grew, so did Cambridge, until today the city that surrounds Harvard is completely built up. There is no more room for random growth. The only solution for both Harvard and Cambridge is better planning for better use of the space available. The three maps show the growth of both Harvard and the built-up part of Cambridge."

The most appreciative attitude toward old buildings is not to surround them with imitations that will put their authenticity in doubt.

A university campus like Harvard architecturally resembles an old cathedral, in the sense that it cannot and should not be a one-style development. The passage of time and the changes it brings should be as much a reality in the visual impact of its architecture as in all other fields of knowledge. Progress is change, in architecture as in anything alive; and a campus has to be alive above all things. This does not mean that the new Harvard buildings should be a vulgar preview of the "world of tomorrow," avowedly sensational and headline-making. Promotional architecture does not belong in a campus; it may find its place in other parts of the city, such as the new downtown skyscrapers, the "glamorous" shopping centers.

Architecture in the campus should be balanced and dignified and should express the courage and forward spirit of a great university. There are some buildings in Harvard that we would call ugly by the standards of taste of 1957. Should they be demolished or "streamlined" to today's taste and the clichés of fashion? Of course not, especially those that are a genuine ex-

Temple University campus model (*Harvard Today*, November 1957, 9). Sert wrote, "Temple University in Philadelphia [planned by Willo von Moltke, working under Edmund Bacon at the Philadelphia City Planning Commission] has many problems in common with Harvard. Like Harvard it is approaching these in cooperation with the city that surrounds it, and one result is the model above. This model contains many features that now exist at Harvard, many that must be included in Harvard's own planning for the future. Among them—preservation of areas of greensward and separation of foot traffic from rushing streams of automobiles."

pression of their time. This gives a particular interest to the campus. It is more alive because of it, and sometimes it is more important to be more alive than more beautiful.

Can we visualize the changes that will take place in the campus? Can we predict them, or shape them?

A pilot plan is only a frame of reference consisting of a series of guiding principles that time will take care to change, because if planning is alive, it has to evolve and adapt itself to changing times and conditions.

The planner does not dictate; his mission is to guide, to make that which is natural more natural. Planning goes with the trends of the times, not against them. Real plans, good plans, are always flexible, adaptable, and actual.

The shape of Harvard cannot be predetermined, but it can be guided, like the shape of a tree.

We can say that we want to keep a certain harmony and scale, improve and multiply the landscaped areas, build high where height is possible or desirable, and try to solve the parking needs without asphalting 50 percent of the campus area. We can say that we want Harvard to be both old and new.

To plan a campus is to foresee, to provide for tomorrow, to put different elements in some kind of order, to classify; and all these efforts should be so directed as to result in a better environment, one which is more congenial to work, study, meditation, and relaxation. Planning is part of teaching, teaching to live better, to see the more beautiful side of life, to enjoy living; and all of it is a form of higher education.

8

THE HUMAN SCALE
KEY TO THE MEASURE OF CITIES (1957)

This appears to be a lecture text delivered to an American Institute of Architects event in Cleveland on April 23, 1957; the title "Cleveland Sprawl" is crossed out at the end of the manuscript. In it, Sert responds to the federal interstate program, approved in 1956, which he recognized would produce "such changes in urban patterns as the world has never witnessed before." In response to the emerging new American metropolitan regions based on interstate highway rather than rail access, Sert argued for the "improvement of daily experience" as the basis of urban design. This talk extended some of the issues raised at the first and second Harvard Urban Design conferences in 1956 and 1957, and carried forward the ideas from his essay, "The Architect and the City," published in Detroit.[1] The urban design implications of these new directions were explored by Sert's Harvard GSD students in various studios, and some of that work was then published in the professional architectural journals.[2]

EM

This country is faced with a radical transformation of its major cities; the Redevelopment Act and the new highway networks are precipitating these changes. If peace and prosperity continue, we may well see, in the next twenty years, such changes in urban patterns as the world has never witnessed before.

The prosperity of the postwar years has brought the development of suburbia to unpredictable sizes. Suburbs joining suburbs along the eastern coast of the United States have made the coastline, from Washington to Boston, appear like one vast metropolis—600 miles long, with a population of 27 million people—and where the only differentiation is one of density: of closeness or scattering of buildings, and where there is no more agricultural land of any considerable size. The whole is probably the largest urban regional complex in the world today. Other vast urban regional complexes have also developed in this country. Cleveland is part of one. I was most impressed with a series of articles published in the *New York Times* some months ago dealing with this subject.

These vast urban regions are shapeless and lacking in scale. The elements of measure existing in the cities of the past—especially those predating the Industrial Revolution—have disappeared. Man is lost in the immensity of these landscapes, which are neither urban nor rural in character. He seems to have been totally ignored in the choice of elements determining their present shapes—walking distances are forgotten, sidewalks tend to disappear, and the few remaining pedestrians are closely watched by police cars in the suburbs of homes for the well-to-do.

What has happened, and what is happening to our cities? What will become of them if prevailing trends continue? The causes that have brought them to this predicament are well known and have recently been carefully analyzed. But what is actually happening is generally overlooked purposely or casually. What may happen in the future is the concern of very few, though it is likely to shape the lives of 170 million people. The government and the majority of people in responsible positions are not doing much about it—let cities continue to sprawl and prosper; the bigger the better! . . . . How long can this laissez-faire attitude last? We have

60 million cars on the road today, we had just 26 million in 1930, and we are expected to have 100 million in the year 1975! You may ask "Who cares for what will happen in the year 2000?" Have you considered that it is only forty-three years away?

You may ask, "What has the car to do with the shape and size of our cities or with their lack of scale?" Some of you are aware of the close relationship; many others may not be. The mechanized means of transportation—first the railroads and subways, then the automobiles—have, together with other innovations of our times, such as mass production and mass merchandising, new methods of food preservation, etc., provoked this tremendous growth of cities. But it is the automobile alone that has permitted the cities to scatter in all directions, bringing people further from one another as it allowed them to commute greater distances along better roads, in any direction, dispersing them also. Real estate speculation could not have developed as it has without the help of the automobile. The automobile has not only transformed the patterns of our cities, it has changed their scale and structure to such an extent that the concept of the city known to us up to [the present] date no longer exists, or is in the process of disappearing; and the urban region has come into being. Can this country let these changes take place without seriously considering where they lead us, what will be the consequences of continued sprawl and growing traffic congestion? In recent times we have heard much talk about decentralization and lower densities as panaceas to the bad conditions prevailing in our cities, but where unplanned decentralization is leading us need not be explained; it is only too evident— it is what we have come to know as urban sprawl, and we are in the midst of it!

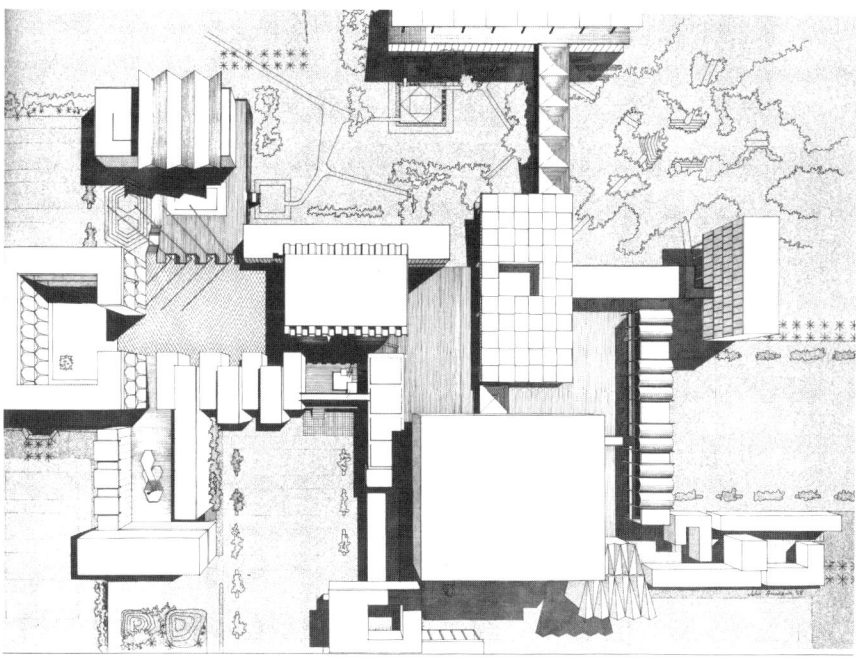

HGSD students, residential sector core for Billerica, Massachusetts. Harvard University Graduate School of Design. *Comparative Housing Study* (1958), 163.

This may be the right moment to explore an approach to the design of cities that takes the more permanent factor as the guiding one. This more permanent factor is the human condition. It is the improvement of our daily existence that should govern our plans. The machines, everything progress has brought us or will bring to us, automation, atomic energy for peace use, etc., are but changing factors on the wide road to progress. In the cycle of the liberation of man, the more permanent factor is the human condition, the nature of man himself, which we cannot radically change.

Sert, sketch of human-scale elements, Chimbote, circa 1947.

In comparison to the Egyptians of 3000 B.C., or the Greeks of the fifth century, man today has changed in essence very little. The human step, the angle of vision or that of the turning of our heads, our reactions to extreme temperatures, to noises, or to the kind of air we breathe are permanent factors—part of human nature. The changes operating during the cycles of our lives from childhood to old age—the need for sleep and rest, love, leisure, and movement, for human ties and for direct human contact, and for those of man to nature, the twenty-four-hour cycle that governs our lives—are basic and as long-lived as man himself. No atomic helicopter will ever replace an apple tree!

Why then not try to shape our cities by those more permanent factors? They may well give us the right answers to many of the problems we should try to solve.

We are aware that if we want to give any kind of shape to urban sprawl, order, measure, and scale, which are the essence of design, should, in some way, be brought to these urban regions.

I believe that we should find new flexible patterns for these regions. Let us then try to guide the waters of the urban flood, as we cannot stop it. The example of flexibility in growth is to be found in nature around us; but natural growth—and I am thinking of plant growth—is not disorderly growth because it is growth by cells that form elements of parts. It is organic growth. The patterns resulting from such growth could produce an urban constellation.

I believe that in such a structure, an urban and urbane way of life can be developed. But the key to such a way of life lies in the preservation of human contacts, and consequently the re-establishment of the human scale; and this calls for the breaking up of these vast regions into urban sectors of differentiated units.

Sert and Jaqueline Tyrwhitt, photographic diagram of sectors in an urban region linked to a parkway. From *The Shape of Our Cities* (unpublished selection of readings and illustrations, 1958), Section 5A, "Man and the Automobile," illustration 34.

These sectors would develop around cores, and the process would be one of groupings around cores or of recentralization as against decentralization. Elements most closely tied to the human scale should influence the design of such sectors.

What is normal in the human environment would find a place in such sectors. Open spaces and trees would be near us and easily accessible. The automobiles also would be within easy reach. Through well-designed parkways that would not cross any populated area, we could move from one unit to another. Roads and parkways would run between townships without interfering with the pedestrian and mechanized movements in their interior, and elements along those parkways would be designed for another scale, that of the automobile.

The whole structure of the agglomerations would become treelike in pattern, the relationship of clusters to roads being similar to that of leaves and branches. Would this then mean the destruction of the city, of its closeness and compactness, of its living together possibilities and closer human contacts? I do not believe so, as it is not distances but time and human energy that matter.

The economy of time in the daily displacement trips is of the greatest importance, as traveling, no matter how good the conditions, adds a considerable part of a day, and consequently of a life and the use of human energy. The long drive besides could be the exception and not the rule if the place of work (daily displacement) is close to residence, in the same township or in one nearby.

We may not have to go to the core of the big metropolis every day, or even regularly; but someday you will want to see a good show on Broadway or have a good meal in Chinatown, at the Chambord, the Colony Club . . . or see a museum opening at the Museum of Modern Art or the Metropolitan, or hear a concert at Carnegie Hall or an opera at the Met, or see the best game of the year or a group of friends in Greenwich Village or . . . . or . . . and this only the big core can provide for. Then you should be able to go easily to the big magnet center, the main core. It will not be too great an effort—if you can get there in a short time, and if you can park your car once you arrive. Again it is *time*, not *distance*, that counts!

All this may be possible if we can in some way reorganize the city; but a radical change in its structure—physical, economic, and political (*New York Times*)—seems the only way out. If in our new urban regional complexes we can establish a network of roads along which traffic can move steadily at a constant speed, this would be the *link road system or main arterial system* to which all sectors connect in some way. Distances outside the main system are then necessarily short—their scale being determined by that of the sector (of 25,000 to 75,000 population). Let us suppose that we leave our home for the main core for any purpose. We would have a short, slow driving distance to cover before getting to the highway, another short distance of slow driving after leaving it, and a very short walk from parking lot to destination—let's say on Broadway, New York.

The main arterial system should be determined considering its function of linking sectors. Now our main highways cut in all directions, and it looks as if in the near future people will be condemned to live, work, and play in the *left-over spaces* between roads. *The trend is to give a priority to the superhighways.* Is this reasonable? I do not believe so, because a highway, like a water main or sewer, electric, or subway line, is a utility, a linking service, a service only, no matter how important.

The actual living, working, or playing spaces, their shapes and size, their relationships, are much more important and should be given priority rating. They are what really shape our way of life and in turn determine the shape of our cities.

If the human factor is properly considered, it is not only the larger elements that will determine that shape, but also the smaller ones. If we have to design a new city, the basic diagram will, it is true, be determined by the main road lines linked to the geographic and topographic conditions—*the constant elements* put by nature on the site, such as rivers, hills, and mountain ranges, and passages between them, harbor and rail facilities, swamps, etc. On the other hand, we cannot forget that all our cities were composed of cells of different types of shelters—for residential use, work, commerce, play, study, or worship—and each of these is in close contact to man, shaped by man, scaled to his spiritual and physical needs. It is the clusters of these cells or shelters, and the spaces between them and around them, that we have come to call our cities.

In an economy like ours, where land is becoming increasingly costly, where space is a rare luxury, in a country increasingly urbanized, *the measuring of space and its careful scaling should develop into a new art,* which is really the art of city design, primarily concerned with measure and scale.

Let us suppose that we have determined the basic diagram for a city, operating from the larger scale. We should then proceed to build up from the opposite end, from the types and groups of cells that will finally determine the sector units that can be distributed along the basic lines of the diagram, linking the whole.

Sert House, Cambridge, Massachusetts, 1958.

Man's needs, spiritual and physical, will shape the elements that govern the shelter-cells, which, in turn, are those that determine the different types of clusters.

So, let us first analyze the cells themselves. Our cells are simply space enclosures, air containers (air conditioned for our greater comfort), enclosed spaces protected from the inclemencies of the open spaces that surround them. The degree of controls can vary from that of simple shelters from rains and wind to those with strictly controlled temperatures, humidity, noises, light, etc.

Their purposes are of the greatest variety—for living accommodations of different standards and different family groups; for permanent living or transient populations; for places to work, such as offices, shops, factories, places of study; for meeting places, public or private; for places of amusement or for places of worship.

But they should all be shaped for human use, for men to move in or live in. All have in common walls, divider screens, doors, windows, storage units, domestic or other machines, furniture, equipment, and useless objects for our delight and pleasure. The necessary and the superfluous—all that is dear to man—have a place in them.

At one time, relatively recently, the elements forming these shelter spaces were also the accumulation or the result of outmoded, obsolete designs; and the resultant spaces were frequently misshapen by the styles of other times that no longer represent a reality.

For the last thirty years, architects have been cleaning up the Augean stables and have made a careful analysis of a new concept of shelter space, known as contemporary architecture.

The architects have worked on the smaller scale of the building, while the planners, aware of the changes of our times, have explored an analytical and comprehensive approach to our cities and regions never before attempted.

But, a vast no-man's land has remained between the activities of one and the other; and this is the field of urban design.

In order to cover it, some planners should develop more in the field of design and three-dimensional planning and move from the flat, abstract diagrams of the land-use maps into the world of spaces and forms and their relationship. This will bring them down to man and his role in shaping those spaces, and their plans will be transformed by human content and improved by additional human calories.

The architect of the younger generation, in his turn, has become aware that a building unrelated to its environment is a utopia. He is conscious that any building is part of a bigger whole, which greatly determines its shape and character.

Some architects will work on the design of larger sectors of the city. This trend is actually taking place, and there is an increasing number of architectural offices going into the field of urban design. This may take the shape of large shopping centers, urban renewal schemes, large hospital centers, university campuses, or even civic cores.

The architect should be better trained to live up to this new challenge offered to him in the urban design field, and to equip young architects for this task is a requirement of architecture schools. To both architects and city planners, the consideration of and familiarity with human scale and measure seems basic.

The architect familiar with shelter cells knows that all their determining elements should be scaled to man. Ceiling heights, windows, and doors are not only measuring human elements in buildings, but also in cities. The double-hung sash gives a human scale to many parts of New York. This scale is lacking in the more modern sectors formed of layer-cake type buildings, where a peak of dehumanization in architecture seems to have been reached.

Careful studies have been made in measuring space in buildings such as factories, stores, hospitals, hotels, and apartment buildings; types have been established and standards set. But we seem to forget that the measuring of space cannot stop or begin at the entrance of a building; it must extend through the environment as a whole.

The patterns of our cities are wasteful, besides being drab and unattractive. Nobody will benefit in the long run from the prevailing disorder; on the other hand, an attractive environment will bring people and keep them, protect land values, and develop a community spirit. People know a better life when they experience it. *A measured, planned environment will pay.*

If, when we leave a well-designed parkway, we can drive into a planned, differentiated sector, what should we see there? Roads and service roads will bring us to peripheral parking lots or garages. There can be planning along these roads: fences can screen the lower buildings, warehouses, and repair shops, and garages and parking lots can be well designed. There can be signs and billboards also if they are of the accepted standards of measure and harmony.

As we get further inside the sector through an animated but controlled main street with properly grouped shops and squares opening off the street to the residential areas, we should find balanced groups of dwellings, high and low apartments, row houses, and detached houses. High buildings and low may offer agreeable contrasts—the low in compact groups of one or two stories screened behind fences and trees; the higher buildings with open spaces around them.

The use of the elevator would determine a clear contrast of heights between walk-up types and those with mechanized vertical transportation. This establishes two measures in vertical scale, as the automobile or pedestrian distances establish a similar differentiation in the horizontal scale.

Places designed for pedestrian movement inside and outside buildings should, of course, take into consideration the angle of vision, movements of the head, and average eye level. They also have to consider perspective effects and foreshortenings and optical deformations. The

Dallas Morning News headline, January 29, 1958.

lack of consideration of these deformations in our high buildings is disagreeable and shows no concern or knowledge of visual matters.

But we also see all these elements of the urban landscape while moving, and they appear as sequences to our eyes. This involves the element of time. With time come also the effects of light or lighting at different hours of the day or night, sunshine and artificial light transforming this environment and adding variety and interest if properly used. Again, we should not forget that our lives are governed by the twenty-four-hour cycle.

The slow movement of the pedestrian permits enjoyment of detail in buildings and landscaping—details that we can grasp, that can make the whole more attractive—such as flowers near the ground, patterns of leaves in trees, patterns of different design in sidewalks or pedestrian parks, and fountains and running water. On buildings the details might be spots of color, changing reflections and shadows, sculptural effects in both large and small patterns, raised textures and forms, and also, perhaps, elements that can be added to buildings that can change according to the seasons, like plants or trees.

When driving through the township at slow speed, the sequence of views changes, as does the eye level; but roads and sidewalks will, as a rule, be apart, and roadsides can and should be designed to be seen from the car in rapid sequence. The treatment of spaces and details will naturally be different—bolder, posterlike and more simplified; many details are unnecessary. But it is nonetheless the human eye that registers these images, and their scale and disposition has to be conditioned accordingly.

Compactness will be a general characteristic in properly designed cities, as all scattering is wasteful. Like the plan of a modern building, the plans of our cities have to be compact. This does not mean they should only be functional, as that word is usually employed to mean the strictly necessary. Far from that, they should allow for all elements that make for better living, one of which, and not the least, is the enjoyment of open spaces. But open spaces does not mean limitless or shapeless spaces. Those we will find outside the city in primeval areas, farmlands, or large parks.

The city landscape should be really urban—man-made and man-shaped—a backdrop or a stage setting for human beings where architecture and the arts can reign supreme.

These human settings have disappeared from our cities. They have become a setting for cars, smog, and noises; but in the compact cities of other times, such settings existed. The pedestrian street or mall, the public squares and arcades, were places for people to see people and recognize them—places to meet and converse. They were scaled accordingly, so as not to tire eyes or feet and so as to provide for a variety of space sequences. They were planned for climate, to shelter from winds or rains, or to benefit from prevailing breezes. Shops would benefit greatly from such plans; see developments in shopping centers.

Why cannot our cities, when replanned, recover the more human settings older cities once provided? Modern materials, modern machines, new methods of building, and a new approach to design should in no way exclude factors that belong to men of all times, that bring harmony and dignity to our environment—elements that nature put in this world we live in and put them there to live with man.

History of past cultures seems to prove that the formation of an urban pattern expressive of a culture is a long, slow process. The urban scene or landscape is a man-made artifact where

Conklin & Rossant, Butterfield House apartments, 37 West 12th St., New York, 1960. Designed by two alumni of Sert's GSD, who were also the architects of the original sections of the new town of Reston, Virginia, in the 1960s.

all other activities and works of man meet. *The city is the real mother of the arts, and their meeting place.* In the past, beautiful cities have appeared as end products of centuries of progress, mature fruits of a mature culture. Are we approaching such a point? As a confirmed optimist, I believe we may. And this country that is faced with the greatest problems of urban growth will, I am sure, find the answers.

SERT'S NOTES

Arithmetic explains the automobile: Since 1930, motor vehicles have multiplied five times as rapidly as the nation's population; the increase in motor vehicles has been 150 percent, and the population has risen 30 percent. By 1975, motor vehicles are expected to show an increase still twice as high as the population rise. The 1975 forecast: Car registration topping 100 million, or a gain of 51 percent over present totals, and an estimated population of 215 million, a rise of 27 percent. These ratios give only one cause for the traffic headaches. Sharing the blame equally is the lack of planning since the twenties and thirties for a nation on wheels. The automobile has not been fitted into modern urban life. It dominates it, inconveniences it, frustrates it.

This redistribution of commerce around the urban core is merging galaxies of satellite communities. One town's factories and offices have become increasingly dependent on the urban region's homes, banks, shops, theaters, airports, hospitals, and throughways.

"Ten men are too few for a city, a hundred thousand too many. A man is not a man unless he is a citizen. Men come together in cities in order to live, they remain together in order to live the 'good' life—a common life for noble ends. The polis population should be self-sufficient for living the good life as a realizable community, but not so large that a sense of conscious unity is lost." —Aristotle

President Eisenhower openly acknowledged in his economic message to Congress ten days ago that the federal government shared responsibility in seeking to resolve metropolitan problems.

Luther Gulick, president of the Institute of Public Administration, stresses a further need for quick state action. He says that each state must set aside large tracts of carefully and scientifically selected land for future highway, recreational, and living purposes. He maintains that uncontrolled metropolitan growth leads to a "progressive destruction of the human habitat." As one example of the high cost of tardy planning, he cites the $40 million-a-mile arterial highway construction being undertaken in downtown Boston.

The shapes the new cities take will depend on controls of land use now under study by planning boards, interstate conferences, universities, and other experts all over the nation, and upon other factors. The possibility for variety is great in a nation whose present cities run to such extremes as New York, with its skyscraper core, and Los Angeles, a horizontal monster crawling almost endlessly from the sea to the desert to the mountains.

9
ARCHITECTURAL FASHIONS AND THE PEOPLE (1959)

In this Harvard GSD lecture given April 7, 1959, Sert emphasizes that he sees prewar "international style" modernism as a thing of the past. He stresses the importance of climate and structure in contemporary architecture, as demonstrated in his former American Embassy in Baghdad (1955) and his Fondation Maeght in France (1958), as well as in the work of Pier Luigi Nervi, Felix Candela, and Minoru Yamasaki.[1] This was near the beginning of the general questioning of modernism after its seeming triumph in the postwar world, and almost coincides with the end of CIAM declared by Team 10 in Otterlo the following fall.

EM

I will try in this talk to clarify some issues and conflicting points of view lately formulated by different colleagues.

On the whole, I welcome divergence and disagreements, as they may avoid the risk of everybody being in the wrong. That would be the worst that could happen to us all. I also believe that disagreements stimulate discussions and criticism, and constructive criticism is healthy and should be welcomed. We do not take much time to talk about things today. To think and converse has become a lost art. I am old enough (which does not mean I am old at all) to remember the rival discussion of the twenties and thirties, especially those that took place during the CIAM conferences. I remember seeing the cleanup of the twenties and thirties and the reactions to the modern architecture at the time. It is really only since the postwar period that modern architecture, and modern art in general, has gotten official status and has aroused worldwide interest.

Revolutionary changes have a great appeal, especially for the younger generation, and today there is a widespread urge to revolt regardless of the nonexistence of the opposition. There is a trend to revolt just to be different, to attract attention, to make headlines. The big names are so much in these headlines that a great many people dream of repeating or starting over again. Since that now belongs to history and in history revolutionary changes only take place when the conditions call for these changes. The man of genius or great foresight knows how to make the best of these conditions. Revolutions and revolutionary changes in architecture, like in other human activities, have to be timely and appropriate. Revolutionary changes per se will lead nowhere. A continuous and self-perpetuating revolution is nonsense. The conditions in the twenties and thirties stimulated writing manifestos of all kinds, but maybe now the manifesto period is over, and we should do better things than write these documents over again.

It is good and healthy that more people working in our field have an urge to do better things than want to do different things. It is good also that they have a faith in the future of man and the possibility of organizing a better of way of living. It is this period where the architect thinks this way that has produced the best and most creative architecture. Contentment with the existing conditions and conformism have never produced anything worthwhile in architecture or city planning. Though revolt is to go forward, I welcome the emphasis on the less material aspects of architecture that has developed since the war. The trend toward the reunion of arts and the interest of architects in the work of painters and sculptors may contribute to a new vocabulary.

> The contemporary architectural movement in the twenties rested on these main points:
> 1. The definition of new programs of needs in our changing environment, constantly modified by different social and economical conditions.
> 2. The use of new technical means to solve these problems.
> Both of these factors result in new forms, with an emotional quality that would satisfy man's spiritual needs.

What is wrongly labeled the international style began to take shape in those years. I say wrongly labeled because the word "international" is generally used in a derogatory sense. I personally believe that whatever we do today will be greatly international or, better, cosmopolitan in character.

As our means of communication continue to increase, the belated encouragement of national labels goes against the trends of the time.

Sert, Jackson & Gourley, Harvard University Center for the Study of World Religions, Cambridge, Massachusetts, 1959.

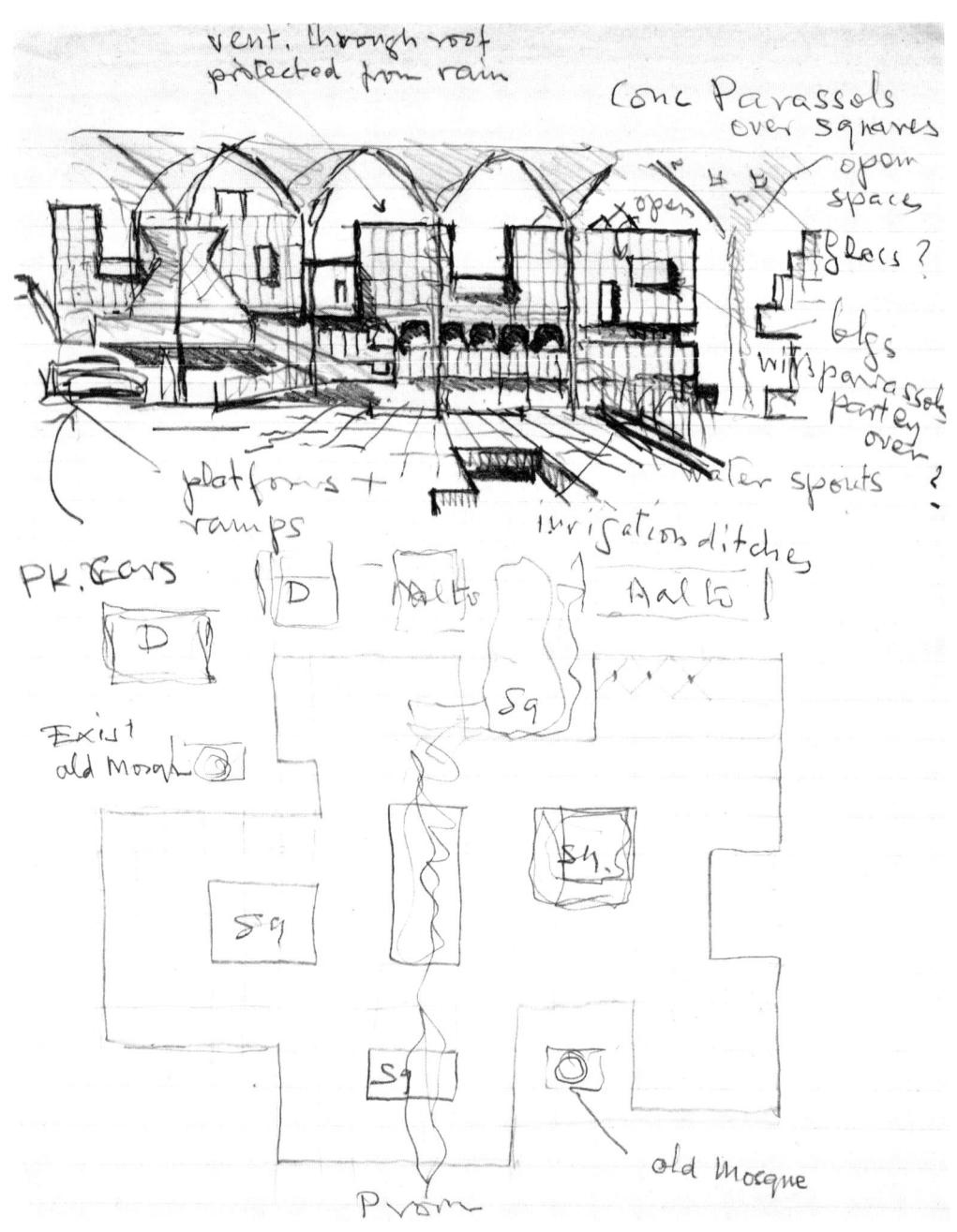

Sert, Baghdad Civic Center sketch, 1955.

The factors determining and shaping our architecture today are mainly those of climate, which have little to do with national boundaries. As the differences in methods of building and use of different materials decrease, our architecture will tend to become more and more cosmopolitan. Certain forms and materials will be typical of tropical, temperate, or cold climates, more than North American, South American, or Western European. The CIAM did not recognize national labels, and the personality of the groups was rather attached to the cities where they worked, the city being a visual reality, while a nation in terms of physical expression is becoming less and less definite.

Since the war there has also been an emphasis on extending the field of architecture into urban design through a closer collaboration with the city planner, the traffic engineer, and other specialists.

There has also been a growing interest in research, and many important developments have taken place in this field. But I want to exchange with you some views on another trend that has developed since the war: the search for a more complete architectural vocabulary, and the widespread statement that modern architecture should drive at functionalism, with a plus factor. Fortunately, form does not necessarily follow function—though it should not be in conflict with it. We recognize today that there is in man an eternal need for the superfluous, if we call superfluous everything that does not correspond to our material needs. The superfluous appears in the first works of man, in the refinement of shape and ornamentation, in the earliest pottery and objects of everyday use.

Minoru Yamasaki, McGregor Conference Center, Wayne State University, Detroit, 1957.

Pier Luigi Nervi, Palazetto dello Sport, Rome, 1958.

The past generations of art critics and historians have made tremendous efforts to try to justify the material or functional intention of any work done by man. There is within us a delight in the useless, and this is already clear in the earliest painters in caves that preceded any buildings. It is necessary to have a faith in a better and more enjoyable way of living, and our physical environment should express this conviction. We may be witnessing a decline of pure materialistic and pseudo-scientific attitude toward life. The architect, like others, works for a better physical environment and should make the best possible use of the scientific and technical progress. But we should not mistake the means for the end.

Architects should make an appropriate use of structure. The help and advice of the engineers is essential to our development. And the architect should give the engineer those things that are the engineer's. I remember Nervi's appropriate statement on this subject. Some architects have developed what we could call a structural complex. There is rather a lacking of interest in the careful studies of modest structures. Yet this seems very important for the better quality of buildings, which are by nature modest.

We do not seem to be able to conceive groups without each building in it trying to outdo its neighbor. The examples of the past show that important buildings are enhanced by the modest and good proportions of those in their neighborhoods.

I think we are by degrees recognizing these matters of relationships between buildings as we develop new views on what our cities should look like. Our cities need a great variety of forms, and this is the coexistence and correlation of these varied forms, open space that will give us better looking cities. We have developed a "versus complex" in the last few years, and there seems to be an attitude to go to extremes and think that certain things exclude others. If we look at the best examples of the past we will find a variety of forms in buildings closely grouped. Different styles often live happily together and make for a better and richer physical environment.

There is rather a dangerous attitude of giving labels to things and making these labels stick, even when they have long been outmoded. Le Corbusier will always be the man of "machine for living" for those who do not understand him or like his work. Though he has long outlived the implications of that statement, others will criticize the unexpected forms of Ronchamp, which do not fit into their picture of the architect. While those that did not like his previous work will hate Ronchamp as the beginning of a new era, which would imply the dropping of all the guiding principles and beliefs of the previous years. Yet it was Corbu, himself, who commented on this subject and told me recently some people would be sorry to see that in the new Brazilian pavilion on the Paris City University campus that he again uses box-like cells, because, as he says, cells are cells and the biology of one building is completely different from another. Corbu, like Picasso, is a great creator of new forms, and if you study his work closely, he, like Picasso, does not contradict himself. The great variety of forms, the greater differences between the work of different architects will only make our cities more exciting to look at. Delight is and will remain part of better living.

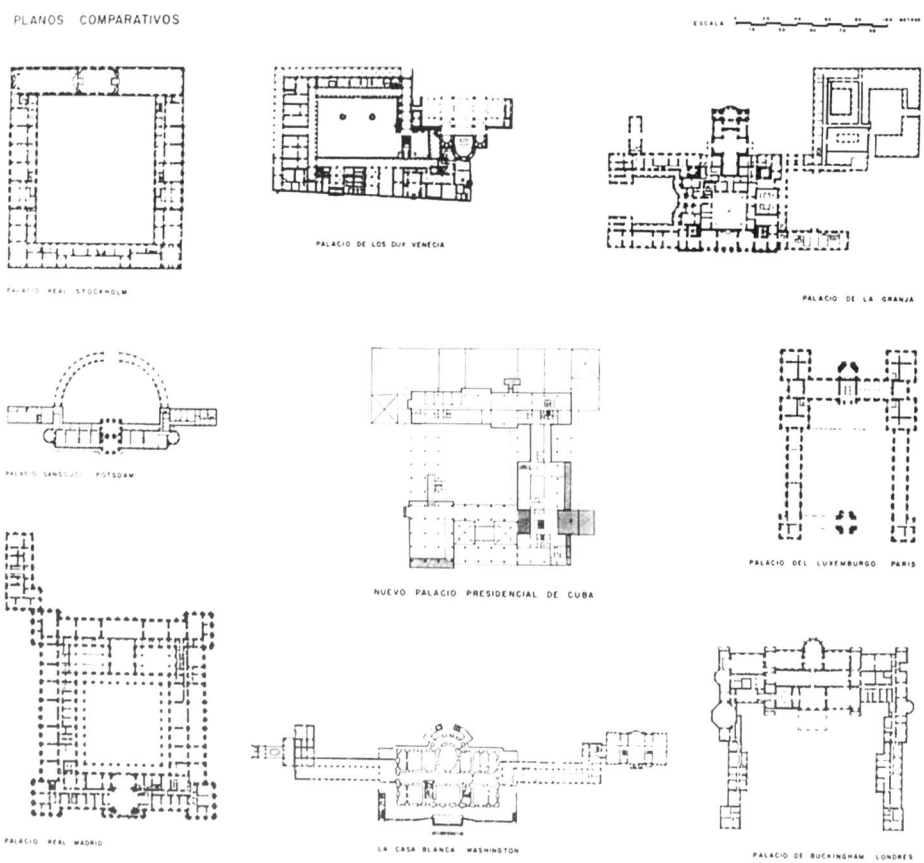

Town Planning Associates, plan comparisons of famous palaces to Sert's presidential palace project, (*Plan Piloto de la Habana*, 1958), an early example of the growing interest in architectural typology by the late 1950s, paralleling the work of Colin Rowe.

Town Planning Associates, with Felix Candela, engineer, presidential palace project, Havana, 1958. View of model. (*Plan Piloto de la Habana*, 1958.)

We tend today to take architecture and the plastic arts too seriously. Our contributions, no matter how good they are, will not save humanity. There is a pathetic urge to do important things against simply agreeable, livable buildings. The press and other media have tended to develop a rather unhealthy genius complex that I hope we will outlive soon, as it is doing more bad than good to architecture in general.

Fashion magazines have influenced architectural magazines that are too often the expression of a rather unhealthy salesman's attitude. Some museums and art critics are unfortunately fomenting this trend.

There is a lack of architectural criticism of the constructive kind. We are menaced by a $300 million civic center that may be a $300 million monstrosity, and no architectural criticism seems to oppose it or expose the facts.

The student councils in the different architectural schools should perhaps make a joint effort to promote one or two really good architectural criticisms that other publications seem unable to undertake. The criticism could also analyze the more stable trends that are now developing in architecture, and serve as guidance to the younger generation of architects. For one good building there are many bad buildings going up in our city, [and] though many interesting things have been done lately, certain types and kinds of buildings are lagging far behind. Many of the changes in our cities do not amount to more than a face lifting operation. They are superficial and do not affect the urban structure in any radical way and will not do much to solve the more critical problems and improve our living.

10
BOSTON
A LIVELY AND HUMAN CITY (1964)

This was first published in the *Boston Globe Sunday Magazine* on March 15, 1964. It coincides with Sert's efforts to advance the efforts of Mayor John Collins and Boston Redevelopment Authority (BRA) director Ed Logue to create a new masterplan for Boston, centered on the redevelopment of City Hall Plaza. Sert was on the advisory board at the BRA, and his firm designed a Catholic chapel for Government Center that was never built. Here Sert calls to the attention of a popular audience the various historical components of Boston's urbanistic successes, while at the same time supporting Logue's effort to create a planned skyline of highrise buildings and other modernist interventions of this still-controversial time.
EM

Boston has joined the great cities in this country in its efforts toward rehabilitation and renewal. Like all living cities, Boston has to change with the times. But these changes need not duplicate those of other cities. Boston has a personality—a past and a future—that is its own.

The character of the city owes much to nature. It has a privileged site: the bay, the harbor, the rolling land beyond. This gives it great advantage over other cities built on shapeless sites or limitless flatlands. Bostonians have improved the beauty of the site through centuries of labor. Some marshlands were filled in as the city spread, creating miles of waterfront; others were flooded and waters were controlled. The Charles River Basin was born.

The park system in Boston is an example that other cities envy. Every measure should be taken to preserve this heritage and continue to expand what we have. The green fingers linking parks should spread as the city is replanned—and no expressway should destroy what was so brilliantly started.

Boston owes as much to the lovers of trees and nature and to the landscape architects as it does to builders and architects. The Commons, the Fenway, Commonwealth Avenue give the city a particular distinction that only many years of labor and care can provide. Frederick Law Olmsted—his work, his ideas, and his influence—contributed greatly to the beauty of our city.

Boston has many interesting and distinguished buildings. The Old State House, Faneuil Hall, the Massachusetts State House, Quincy Market, Trinity Church, and the Boston Public Library are part of a precious heritage. Bulfinch and H. H. Richardson made great contributions in their day; their buildings are all very different but share a particular Bostonian vitality.

But it takes more than isolated masterworks to make a lively city. It is the clusters of groups of fine, well-proportioned buildings, defining streets and squares (Louisburg Square), parks, and water frontages that shape the open spaces and are the face of the city.

The tight building cluster on Beacon Hill, crowned by the gilded dome of Bulfinch's State House, seen in the clear morning sunshine is one of the most beautiful sights the city has to offer.

Back Bay offers a regular plan. It has unity and measure. It has Commonwealth Avenue, which is one of the most beautiful streets in the country. The proportion of the width of the street to the height of the buildings, the center promenade and trees (between Arlington Street and Kenmore Square) make this thoroughfare one of Boston's best features. The architecture may not match that of the small brick row houses on the Hill, but, regardless of details, it has continuity in scale and treatment. It is all in one piece and dates from one period—a rare thing indeed today.

Boston skyline looking east over the Charles River. At right is Sert's Boston University Law and Education Schools tower (Sert, Jackson & Associates with Edwin T. Steffian, with landscape design by Sasaki, Dawson, DeMay, 1964–67), part of the Sert, Jackson campus masterplan. At center is Charles Luckman and Associates' Prudential Center (1959), and at left is I. M. Pei's John Hancock Insurance Company tower (1972–75) in Copley Square.

Charles Bulfinch, Massachusetts State House, 1795–97, with later alterations and additions. Sert wrote in the *Boston Globe Sunday Magazine*, "'Hub of the Solar System' was how Oliver Wendell Holmes once described the State House. Certainly it is the crowning glory of Beacon Hill and for more than 165 years the 'King of Buildings' in Boston. This striking view of the Bulfinch-designed capitol, with its golden dome glistening in the morning sun, [is near] the Boston Bar Association headquarters on Beacon Street."

Alexander Parris, Quincy Market, Boston, 1824-26, renovated by Benjamin Thompson Associates as Faneuil Hall Marketplace, 1976-78. Thompson was chair of architecture during Sert's deanship in the 1960s.

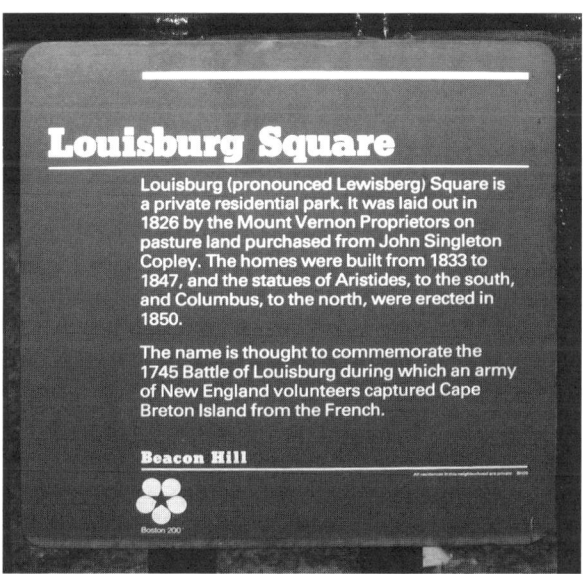

McKim, Mead & White, Boston Public Library, 1888-95. Sert wrote, "Another aristocrat among Boston buildings is the Central Library Building, Copley Square, of the Boston Public Library. An American classic in the Italian Renaissance style, it opened in 1895 and was the first of the great modern library buildings in this country. The seals of the library, the city, and the Commonwealth are over the portals."

Louisburg Square plaque. Sert wrote, "An island sanctuary in the Boston hubbub is famed Louisburg Square on Beacon Hill, with its red brick houses, wrought-iron railings and grillwork balconies facing a charming little park reminiscent of London's regal old squares."

Sert with Boston Catholic Cardinal Cushing and model of Sert's unbuilt Government Center chapel, 1963.

The Charles River Basin, with the three universities on its margins, offers unique possibilities if treated as a visual entity.

So much for the past. But what of the future? Boston is the center or core of a large metropolitan region. Changes have to be accepted whether we like them or not. They are an expression of the vitality and prosperity of the city. The land available is limited, and all of it has been developed and built upon, with the exception of parks and streets. Higher densities can be accepted if land is used more efficiently and intelligently. Densely built areas can be found in many of the most beautiful cities.

Higher real estate taxes and the increasing cost of public services and utilities make careful planning mandatory. The modern means of transportation, the alarming growth of the number of privately operated automobiles, the lack of an adequate public transport system call for a planning organization on the metropolitan scale.

A more intense use of the land in certain parts of the city is, if properly planned, desirable. This has to be related to the new expressway system, as greater building heights should be an

Le Corbusier, with Sert, Jackson & Associates, Carpenter Center for the Visual Arts, Harvard University, 1963. View from the ramp into the art studios. Sert wrote, "Probably the most controversial building built in the Boston area in years is the new Carpenter Center for the Visual Arts at Harvard University. Designed by the great French architect Le Corbusier, and his first building in North America. The Fogg Museum is next door."

expression of the more active sections. New main arteries equipped to feed high buildings can appear as ridges or spines in flatter surroundings. Small clusters of highrises can feed into parking garages, well-linked to the expressways. Waterfront and park fronts are appropriate for such high apartment, office, and hotel buildings, as these face open spaces.

Boston is already growing in height. Can this growth be planned and a certain order established? In the old prints showing the skyline of the city, the church spires, providing the vertical accents to the walkup scale of other buildings, were well spaced and added life and expression to that skyline. At a new and vaster scale, the one imposed by the needs and means of today, a contrasted skyline, is, I believe, possible and desirable.

What has been started is promising. The Government Center provides the needed extension of the core of public buildings around the State House. There will be public spaces, squares, and landscaping in the vicinity—a new City Hall that will be an exciting architectural landmark. Hopefully these spaces can be properly related physically and visually to the renewal of the harbor waterfront, while the North End can be rehabilitated to preserve its liveliness and villagelike character. The new expressways, helping to define its edges, make it a self-contained community.

Other links have to be developed between the Government Center and other parts of the city. Extensions toward North Station, the Charles, and the Washington Street areas will help establish visual ties.

Between the Prudential Center and Fenway areas, the main transportation lines (streets, subways, and new expressways) and Boylston and Tremont Streets call for the establishment of spines of more intense use. The nineteenth-century set an example by linking the Fenway, Commonwealth Avenue, the Common, and the State House on the hill. But the new spines that can be envisioned would have an entirely different scale and magnitude determined by the new requirements and possibilities.

Many new elements will influence the growth and visual image of the city. The NASA project, the expansion of the large complexes of public and educational buildings, and even the projected Boston World's Fair offer a broad field for experimentation in large-scale planning and design ideas.

11
THE ROLE OF GOVERNMENT IN THE FORM AND ANIMATION OF THE URBAN CORE (1964)

Here at the Eighth Urban Design Conference, Sert looks back on the successful series of seven Harvard Urban Design Conferences held since 1956.[1] The two previous conferences, the sixth and the seventh, had been on the theme "Designing Inter-City Growth," with the seventh (1963) focused specifically on "The Shopping Center as a Nucleus of Inter-City Activity."[2] Sert then introduced the first speaker, Robert C. Weaver, then the administrator of the Federal Housing and Home Finance Administration and soon to be appointed the first secretary of Housing and Urban Development by President Lyndon Johnson. In that role, Weaver, a longtime housing activist and a protégé of Catherine Bauer during the New Deal, became the first African-American to hold a Cabinet post.[3]

EM

José Luis Sert, dean of the Graduate School of Design, opened the conference in Sanders Theater on Friday morning, May 1, before an audience of eight hundred, saying:

> I welcome you all here in the name of President Nathan Pusey, who was sorry not to be able to be with us to open this conference.

We have now come to the eighth in our series of Urban Design Conferences, which started in 1956. After two years spent in exploring the outer fringes of urban development, we are now returning to our original area of interest, the central city. Our first two conferences dealt with general aspects of urban design, then quite a new concept. But at our third conference, in 1959, we adopted a case-study system and we have retained it ever since. This has meant that each conference has had a special theme which has been discussed in small panels with reference to actual concrete examples.

In 1959, our first subject was the design of large-scale residential projects in downtown areas, and this was followed by a conference on civic institutions as generators of urban form. Both these treated case studies from inner-city areas, using examples from Chicago, Detroit, New York, Philadelphia, St. Louis, and Toronto, as well as Cambridge and Boston.

However, several members of our alumni council, which takes an active part in the preparation of these conferences, had always felt that our main problem in America lies in our vast inter-urban stretches of suburbia that now tend to carpet all the land between cities in the major metropolitan areas of this continent. Our last two conferences have therefore been devoted first to the whole problem of orderly and satisfactory methods of designing for intercity growth, and secondly, last year, to the phenomenon of regional shopping centers as possible foci of intercity activity.

At this conference there was a general feeling that we were, at best, discussing a poor substitute for the lively and viable city center, and that it was time we returned to the city to see how far present programs of urban renewal could enable it to resume its traditional role as the cradle of our civilization, the place where all the most progressive thought and experiment can be openly felt and expressed, and can be criticized and evaluated in terms of our historic past: new developments in art, music, and theater, as well as new developments in scientific discovery and administrative methodology.

This was the sequence by which we arrived at the topic of our present conference: "The Role of Government in the Form and Animation of the Urban Core." This title was carefully chosen after much debate, and the omission of the actual words "urban design" and "urban renewal" was deliberate. We have also selected, for the first time, a single city as our case study: the core of the metropolitan area of Boston. And within this core, we are confining ourselves to four particular aspects, which we believe to represent crucial problems in many other metropolitan cities of the country. These will form the subject of discussion for four panels which will meet throughout this afternoon and tomorrow morning. The first panel deals with the design of Boston's government center area in relation to the form and animation of Boston's urban core, considering particularly the role played by government in bringing this about.

Proposed renewal of the Boston waterfront by the Boston Redevelopment Authority, 1964. From Wolf van Eckhardt, "Architectural Commentary on Boston Today," *Ekistics* 18-105 (August 1964): 9.

The second panel is studying the part played by major downtown institutions in the city of the future, and in Boston this refers especially to hospitals and universities. Our third panel is handling the design of downtown residential areas under the urban renewal program, and examining their present and possible contribution to the form and animation of the city. Finally, the fourth panel takes a look at the form and expression of the entire urban core of Boston as the culmination point of the metropolitan area it serves: How far is this fact and this image being promoted and assisted by the present administration of public funds? Is there anything we can suggest to assist the federal government to act more effectively in this area?

This brings me to my final point, our hopes for the outcome of this conference. Until now, our urban design conferences have worked very quietly and only issued short reports of our internal discussions, which have sometimes been reprinted in the technical press and sometimes simply been distributed among ourselves.

When we started in 1956, urban design was not only a novel concept, it was also highly suspect in many quarters. But today the atmosphere is different. The term "urban design" has come into common use and is seriously discussed—though with various shades of meaning—at all levels of government and in all schools of architecture and city planning.

Therefore, this year we hope to come up with something more than simple reportage. As stated in our first communiqué, our four panels have the responsibility of attempting to "arrive at a restatement of federally supported urban renewal's public goals and project approach; to view their compatibility with private goals; and to recommend procedures to give effect to this restatement. It is intended that our conference resolutions shall be pointed and capable of administrative implementation. It is thought that they may include statements concerning the sequence and descriptive characteristics of the steps necessary to establish soundly conceived and imaginative urban design being incorporated in the urban renewal process from its earliest stages."

As evidence of the direct government interest taken in our efforts, we are most honored and delighted to have with us the man who is head of the nearest thing we have to a department of urban affairs, as yet: Mr. Robert Weaver, administrator of the Housing and Home Finance Administration. Also, this morning we hope to hear an objective critique of the changing face of downtown Boston, much of which results from the employment of federal funds, from a Washington critic, Mr. Wolf Von Eckardt. Finally, we shall give the floor to the director of the Boston Redevelopment Authority, Mr. Edward Logue. I now have the pleasure of introducing our first speaker, Mr. Robert Weaver.

12
OPEN SPACES AND PEDESTRIAN PATHS IN THE UNIVERSITY (circa 1960s)

This undated text is an excerpt from *Harvard University, 1960: An Inventory for Planning*, a Sert-led effort to document the campus environment and its history, and to produce what then became a partial basis for much of the university's development in the 1960s. It explains in detail how Sert's pedestrian-based urban design concepts could be systematically applied to the Cambridge campus.

EM

> A man's eyes cannot be as much occupied as they are in large cities by artificial things . . . without a harmful effect. . . . An influence is desirable that, acting for the eye, shall be antithetical, reversive and antidotal. Such an influence is found in what will be called the enjoyment of pleasing scenery.
> —Notes on *The Plan of Franklin in Park*, 1886, Frederick Law Olmsted

The development and landscaping of open spaces is essential in the life of any community, and especially in that of a university. The Old Yard was the first open space that Harvard developed. It is the core of the university community. It is an unbuilt space shaped by buildings. Like the village green in the old New England towns, it is a symbol of community life, of togetherness. With the growth of the university, the yards have multiplied to meet these needs for open space, the same way buildings are provided for enclosed space of different kinds.

As traffic conditions have changed radically with the appearance and increase of automobiles, cities have lost their once-green squares and tree-lined avenues. Hard-top surfaces are rapidly replacing them to meet the urgent needs for increased parking facilities. Asphalt replaces grass, trees are often considered a luxury and a nuisance. Immediate material considerations have brought about the sacrificing of the beauty and livability of communities. But we are quickly becoming aware that such green spaces and places of quiet are a must in any community, especially in a university.

The increased congestion around the Yard makes such spaces even more necessary, and they should multiply as the university expands. It is important that pedestrian movement be made easier and more agreeable, and this requires that the green quadrangles be linked by tree-lined paths and malls, the whole providing a pedestrian network that can be independent from the traffic network, both meeting only at certain exchange points and crossings and accesses to buildings.

Against the trends of the times, the university has had the courage and wisdom to prevent the invasion of the yards by automobiles. This is a proof of the importance it attaches to the safeguarding of the human factors that enhance a community. In moments when the prevailing trends seem to overlook these factors, *universities should set an example that may influence cities to change their attitude* and make them aware of the urgent need to safeguard and develop a planned network of green spaces.

As the city of Cambridge develops its masterplan, the university may become the center of a clearly defined area limited by the new expressways. The park system of that part of the city can be linked with that of the university proper. This would facilitate pedestrian movement from the center to the fringes of such an area.

HARVARD UNIVERSITY

The University established an 'Office of the Planning Coordinator' in 1957. The architect was appointed consultant to this office. A study of existing University plans was made and a system of unified presentation was devised. The University did not want a rigid master plan; it only requested guidance and coordination in its development so that its land and resources would be efficiently put to the best use.

Harvard University is an important sector of a city of one hundred thousand people, the City of Cambridge. The planning office from the very start tried to plan the development of the University in close relationship with that of the City. The architect had been chairman of the Cambridge Planning Board for one and a half years; this gave him a thorough knowledge of the problems of the City, which was then discussing a new plan and several urban renewal and redevelopment projects.

Cambridge is an important sector of metropolitan Boston, where a general highway system is under construction. This system consists of several radial expressways and two belt roads – the inner and the outer belt. Cambridge, and consequently Harvard University, will be greatly affected by this new expressway system which will alleviate congestion in Harvard Square (core of the commercial sector) establishing a by-pass for through-traffic. The University may become the core of a sector, its limits well defined by the expressway system.

Like all universities in the United States, Harvard has to face the problems brought by growth. But, being in the center of an entirely developed city (with less than ten per cent of open land), its campus is an urban campus, a city within a city, and it is faced with the traffic congestion, lack of parking spaces, high cost of land, etc., which any community of its size would encounter.

From its very beginnings the University has built a series of quadrangles or yards, groups of buildings defining open landscaped spaces. The Office of the Planning Coordinator tried to continue this pattern of development wherever possible and appropriate, providing access and parking facilities on the periphery of these quadrangles.

The green spaces, or quadrangles, were not only extended but linked by green pedestrian lanes, making a continuous pedestrian path system or network of the whole. The scarcity of land and the fact that University property is tax-exempt make it advisable (in the interest not only of the University but also of the City of Cambridge) that the land available be put to maximum use. High-rise blocks, properly spaced and sited, are one answer to this intense land-use requirement. Garages will have to replace parking on grade. Many of these changes may not be ideal, or even desirable, but they are requirements of our changing times – they will allow the University to keep the open green spaces and even extend them. The margins of the Charles River provide good sites for high-rise buildings and, if these are properly related and spaced, they can help define this space and add the needed accents. This approach has been followed in Holyoke Center which is part of a business zone, and in the Married Student Dormitories on the Charles River.

Sert and Harvard University Planning Office, Harvard University pedestrian pathway system, circa 1960. Sert founded the planning office in 1955, directed by GSD alumnus Harold Goyette, and published *Harvard University, 1960: An Inventory for Planning,* which explained the concepts in this essay in more detail.

View of Holyoke Center from Harvard Yard.

THE EXISTING CONDITIONS

These consist of public open spaces, large and small open spaces of unique design characteristics belonging to the university, and a series of paths—public and university—which connect these together.

Some of the Harvard spaces are classics of their kind; others need to be strengthened as design forms. More of all categories should be constructed as part of any long-range development plan.

PUBLIC OPEN SPACES

Harvard is fortunate in having many pleasant open spaces within walking and viewing distance. Though the public use of these spaces should not be impinged on, careful consideration should be given to the visual use of the amenities.

This is particularly true of the Charles Riverbank, where public access must be provided. At the same time, however, the design value of this open space should be accounted for in any siting of buildings, or in relating other sectors of the campus to this natural focal point.

CAMPUS SPACES

A campus space can be described as a space that contains three or more buildings, has boundaries that can be sensed and related to the human scale, and which is undivided by vehicular through traffic. The Harvard Yard is the classic example in this category, the Radcliffe Yard is another. These spaces provide a logical design context for such things as:

a) functional use areas;
b) siting a known building program yet providing for expansion;
c) large-scale landscape effects;
d) linking together dissimilar functional areas into a recognizable design form;
e) controlling traffic and parking.

SECTOR SPACES

These spaces are related to particular building groupings and are part of the natural extension of the architecture. They may be part of the open space pattern of the Campus Space, or could be individual units. Examples of the former are the spaces around Holden Chapel [see page 73], in back of Sever Hall, or in front of the Biological Laboratories. Examples of the latter are the green areas in Mather Courtyard, or the space around Memorial Hall and Sanders Theatre. Sector spaces can be as big as the two quadrangles that comprise the Yard, or as small as the green area in front of Apthorp House. These spaces should never be penetrated by other than emergency vehicles and should be landscaped in a manner appropriate to their architecture and use.

PRIVATE SPACES

Private spaces are small landscaped areas with access limited to those who live in or use the architecture to which they are related. Private spaces at Harvard range from the area in front

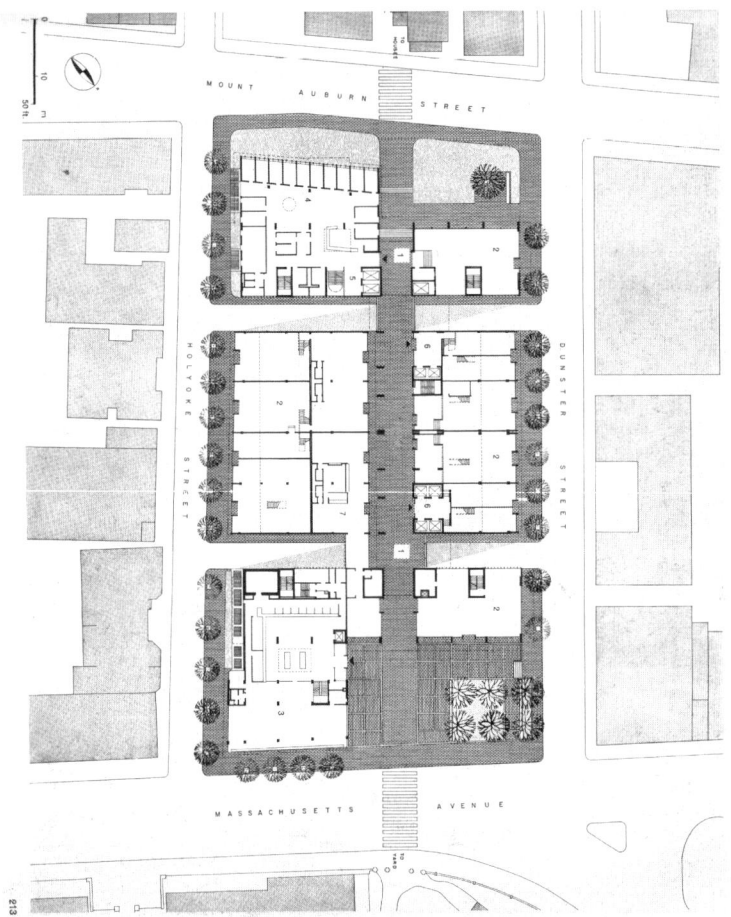

Sert, Jackson & Gourley, Holyoke Center (Harvard University Administration Building), 1958–65. Plan of first level with pedestrian walkway, enclosed in the 1990s.

Apthorp House, Cambridge, Massachusetts, 1760, now part of the Harvard University campus.

SBRA (Shepley Bulfinch Richardson and Abbott), Quincy House, Harvard University, 1955-59.

of the president's house to the intimate courtyards and roof garden belonging to the Master Tutors of Quincy House.

Such spaces are psychologically important in the university environment, for they relieve the conflict between the sheer size and public use character of the physical plant and the natural inclinations of individuality that are a part of the Harvard tradition. These spaces should be included in the architectural programs for all new buildings, residential as well as teaching and research facilities—partially, perhaps, as an extension of the interior architectural space.

PLAY FIELD SPACE

Play fields are of two kinds: those whose use can be scheduled and evaluated as teaching facilities or part of the university's athletic program, and informal play space whose use is unpredictable and tied to whim and fancy—hour, and seasonal and personal vagaries. On the Cambridge campus, the construction and maintenance of play fields seems economically prohibitive and politically unfeasible. How much of this space should be held south of the Charles River depends on the university's educational policies. There are no known universal standards to this respect.

Because the university operates an extensive intramural program and because of the urban land values of its Cambridge property, it would seem appropriate to give informal playfield space a low priority in any development plan.

UTILITY SPACES

Utility spaces are those areas used primarily for service and parking. Since separation of vehicular traffic from pedestrian traffic is an accepted principle in institutional planning

Sert, Jackson & Associates, Harvard University Science Center, 1968—73.

today, public use of these spaces will become increasingly linked over a period of time. As such, their design treatment should be related to maximum efficiency in function and maintenance. Their landscape should be appropriate to the use to which they are put, with little, if any, embellishment. This means they should not be ignored, but recognized for that they are. Where possible, pedestrian traffic should be kept out of these spaces.

MAJOR AND SECONDARY SPACES

Greenways are landscaped paths of movement. Major greenways carry vehicular and pedestrian movement, while minor greenways are designed for the exclusive use of the pedestrian, though occasionally emergency and service vehicles can be carried. Major greenways are landscaped for three purposes:

a) to create strong design "lines" which can be used to differentiate various categories of streets, or to serve as boundaries, etc., etc.;
b) to reduce and control the noise of vehicular traffic;
c) simply as an amenity, something pleasant for the driver and the pedestrian.

Boylston Street from the Charles River to Winthrop Street and Divinity Street are examples of major greenways. Secondary greenways at Harvard are mostly informal in their design, and have grown mostly by chance.

THE PROPOSED CONDITIONS

The proposed system will establish links between the existing and proposed yards; these will be pedestrian paths and malls. There is the possibility of establishing two north-south paths that would allow pedestrians to move from the Business School area to that of the Law School and Harkness Commons. One follows Holyoke Street and crosses the Old Yard; the other, starting at the same point, would link De Wolfe Street, enter the Old Yard area near Lamont Library, cross the Yard from Widener Library to Appleton Chapel (Memorial Church), and pass behind Memorial Hall up Divinity Avenue toward the Peabody Museum and Andover Hall. These two north-south paths could be linked with others branching out from them and following an east-west direction. These are:

a) Soldiers Field Road, linking the Business School buildings, the Stadium and the proposed married students housing on the Charles;
b) Dunster Street, Mill Street, and Grant Street, paralleling the Cambridge side of the Charles River, linking the old and new houses extending from the MTA rail yards on the west to the Houghton School urban renewal area on the east;
c) Along the interior of the block between Massachusetts Avenue and Mount Auburn Street;
d) From the commons on Massachusetts Avenue through the Old Yard to the Fogg Museum's sculpture garden and the new Design Center [Le Corbusier's Carpenter Center];
e) From the Law School yard to the Peabody Museum, the Divinity School, and the old married students' apartments on Shady Hill.

Sert, Jackson & Associates, Peabody Terrace Married Student Housing, Harvard University (1963) on the Charles River, looking east.

Other pedestrian links across the Cambridge Common could tie the Yard to the Radcliffe quadrangles and the Loeb Drama Center on Brattle Street. These green spaces and paths could be varied in shape and character and serve different needs. Pedestrian arcades protecting from heat and rain are a useful element; if walking is made easy and agreeable, it can help reduce car parking in and around the more central areas of the university. One such arcade will be provided by the Health Center and office block; others may follow. Encouraging pedestrian movement may help reduce parking problems and traffic congestion.

With the growth of the university and the development of the Charles Riverbank, there is no doubt that the open space system should find a design climax around the open space provided by the river. Highrise buildings logically belong there, and they will require plenty of open space between them. They should not be clustered like the downtown office buildings but widely spaced, like the bell towers of the old churches. Between towers, lower walk-up structures with sunny courts can maintain the scale of the old Cambridge unchanged. The old can, and should, live with the new.

13

SIGFRIED GIEDION IN MEMORIAM (1968)

Written after Giedion's death, this text outlines the Swiss architectural historian's importance to modern architecture, including his pivotal role in organizing CIAM (1929–56) and in aiding the growth of the Harvard GSD under Sert's deanship (1953–69).
EM

I made Sigfried Giedion's acquaintance in the late twenties. I saw him frequently in the Congrès Internationaux d'Architecture Moderne (CIAM) and at preparatory meetings, then later in New York during the war years, and finally at Harvard in our joint work at the Graduate School of Design. Giedion had a unique personality and was a man of varied interests: in architecture, in engineering, in cities, in the visual arts and their relationship in life in general, and in good food. During the war years in Long Island we discussed many of these subjects and shared many a good meal with friends such Fernand Léger, Alexander Calder, Jacques Lipchitz, Walter Gropius, and Amédée Ozenfant.

Giedion was a discoverer of a recent but unknown past; and he often used to comment on the lack of interest and appreciation or effort to document the recent inventions and discoveries that have shaped our industrial civilization. He was shocked to learn that the U. S. government authorized the sale of the National Patent Office collection of scale models and documents, which represented some of the most significant inventions and creative ideas in home and office furnishings and equipment of buildings that have shaped much of the environment in this country. Of this he said, "They want to build new museums and have here assembled the best material for a uniquely American museum—yet they let it be dispersed."

Sigfried Giedion has written some of the most important architectural books of this century. His best known work, *Space, Time and Architecture* [first published in 1941], has given students a better understanding of the world we live in. Some American documents had never before been published. Giedion discovered them because he was concerned with the origins of the things around us. He was a man who lived in the present, although he investigated the past. He understood the relationships between the visual arts; he extended architecture to building technology and to city planning and urban design when such broad views were shared by only very few. All developments in the arts were for him one continuous process as it related with architecture, urban design, and the visual arts and was formulated in his series of remarkable books on *The Eternal Present* (in two volumes, *The Beginnings of Art and The Beginnings of Architecture*, prepared with the assistance of Jaqueline Tyrwhitt and published in 1964).

Giedion's approach is always personal and unconventional. He had the gift to discover many facts that had been overlooked or ignored by other art historians. In the last weeks of his creative life he finished *Architecture and the Phenomenon of Transition*, completing his three space conceptions in architecture.

He had wanted to write a brief history of the International Congresses [CIAM]. He had been the secretary of this group from its inception in 1928, at the Chateau de la Sarraz. For twenty-six years he gave the Congresses his enthusiastic, unpaid help, and his family in Zurich had sacrificed

Giedion and Sert, undated postwar photo.

Sigfried Giedion House, Zurich. Giedion, born in Prague and trained as an engineer and as an art historian under Heinrich Woefflin in Munich, lived here on the Zurichberg for many years with his wife, the art historian Carola Giedion-Welcker. Giedion had a central role in the development of both modern art and CIAM (International Congresses for Modern Architecture).

a room in their house in the Doldertal to store the collection of documents that Giedion never had the time to select or destroy. The Zurich Polytechnic Institute will be the depository of those papers after the history of CIAM is published as an homage to Sigfried Giedion.

Giedion had the youthful mind of the discoverer—he was very close to the young people of today, and the students who know and appreciate sincerity loved him and will miss him. In the Graduate School of Design at Harvard, where he taught for many years, he devised a new approach to teaching the history of architecture based on the changing conceptions of space, and organized a unique seminar in urban planning, making these subjects alive and meaningful to the younger generations.

14

ARCHITECTURE AND THE PEOPLE
THERE ARE TWO HISTORIES OF ARCHITECTURE (1972)

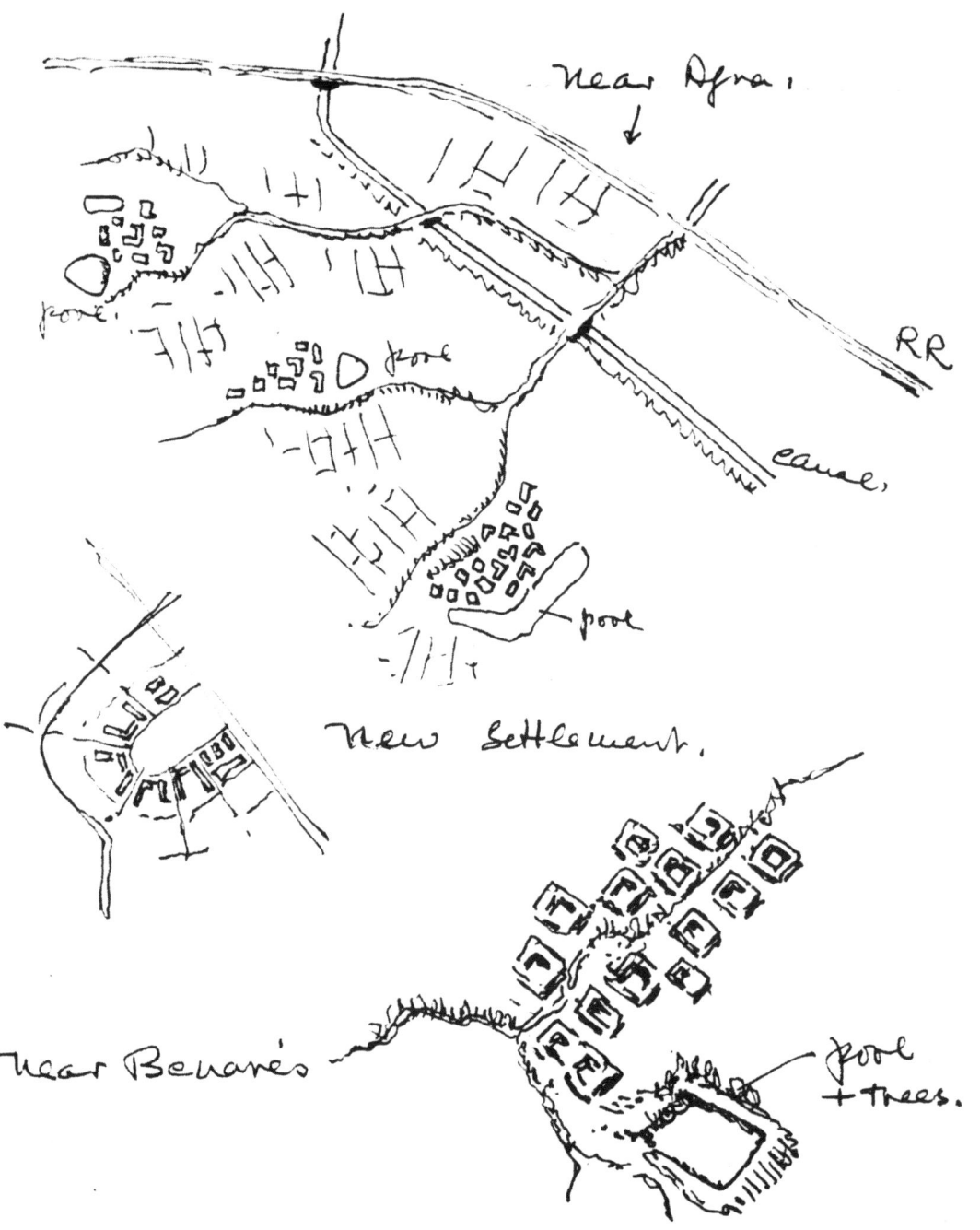

Sert, sketches of new settlement and settlement patterns near Banares and Agra, India, circa 1970.

In this lecture given at the Museum of Fine Arts, Boston, after his retirement as dean of the GSD in 1969, Sert reiterates his long-held belief in the validity of the vernacular as a source of direction for contemporary architecture. He mentions, in addition to his usual Mediterranean references, his firm's efforts to create what would now be called a sustainable resort community for the Frioul Islands, off the French coast from Marseille, an example of a car-free, dense environment. He also cites Bernard Rudofsky, who organized the influential 1964 Museum of Modern Art exhibition "Architecture without Architects," on the importance of pedestrian "streets for people."
EM

There are two histories of architecture.

One dealing with the more ambitious buildings constructed to the glory of gods, kings, or tyrants, or representing governments or the big corporations . . . Another, still partly unwritten, that should deal with the styleless anonymous structures, the architecture that people themselves built for the people.

These kinds of buildings, simple, honest, unpretentious, that when grouped have given us the towns of the Greek islands, the hill towns of Italy, the old New England communities. This architecture and the plans in general are timeless—visually, they are as alive today as when they were born.

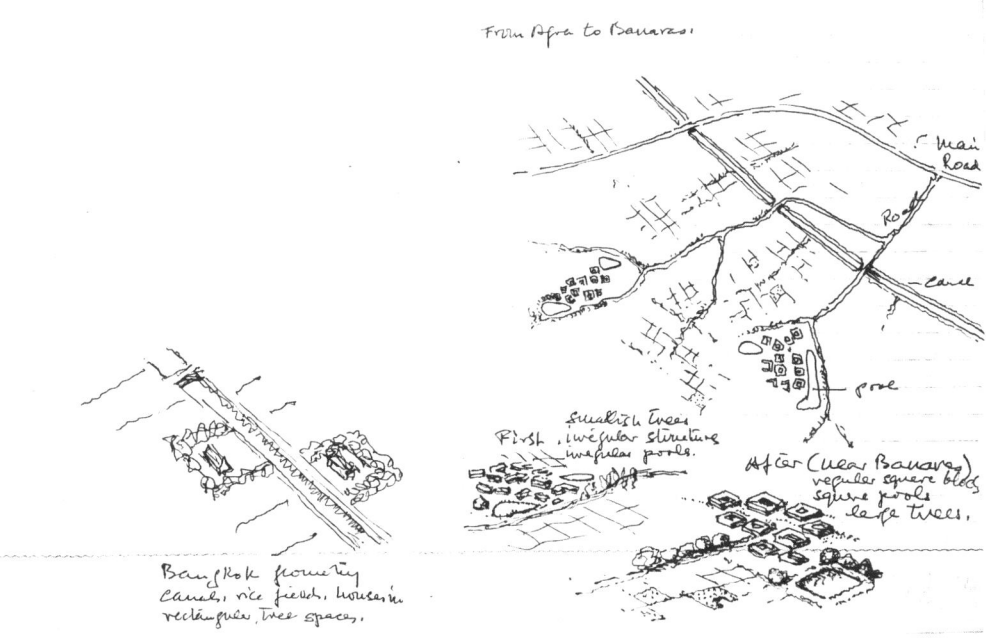

Sert, sketches from Thailand and India, circa 1970.

127 ARCHITECTURE AND THE PEOPLE

Many young architects discovered such towns after the last great war or while serving their countries abroad.... They were moved by the liveliness and spontaneity of such buildings—by their gaiety and human quality, by the harmonious clusters or groupings of buildings, by the expression of a natural process of growth resembling that of nature.

They compared them to the dreariness of the functional, overdesigned products of the big architectural offices, which looked dead. They are visually dead and have the rigidity of death (rigor mortis).

That is why many of the overdesigned buildings produced today, products of careful analysis and thinking, complying with outmoded codes and zoning regulations, are rejected by the people. They naturally do not listen to arguments but just want to enjoy and live in buildings.

Which are the conditions that have given birth to the monstrosities that proliferate in our cities?

I remember Le Corbusier, whom I was privileged to work with, commenting when he was shown a modern overdesigned project: "L'architecture n'est pas si difficile que ça ... " ["But architecture is not as difficult as that ... "]

The anonymous architecture of the people confirms this statement. But it is true today that it is very difficult to do things simply, naturally, well—and be good. Which are the obstacles to the easy? Or the apparently easy ... ?

> The complexities of the urban picture.
> The artificial, man-made barriers.
> The clash between machines and machine-made products and nature and natural forms.
> — The mechanical insides of buildings, their increased complexity and cost (35 to 70 percent).
> — The limitations imposed by these complexities.
> — The lack of a real building industry. We are living through a period of transition.
> — The limitless greed of the land speculators. Land is unused, held for higher prices—or abused, overbuilt, and exploited. It is not considered in terms of its possible livability but of its possible exploitation—its marketability.

Land should really be taxed when it is unused or when it is abused. Proper, rational use should be encouraged by lowering taxation, as it represents an economy in city finances.

The shapes or shapelessness of our cities today are an expression of the forces that give birth to them. They are the horrible but natural product of the seeds we sow ...

The skyline parallels (or corresponds to) land prices (costs) at street level. It expresses the points of greater congestion.

The use and abuse of the private automobile in the heart of the city has accelerated the process of disruption. The efforts and cost of this absurdity are only too evident.

Kasbah Fadala, Tunisia, undated aerial photo in the Sert archive, Harvard Graduate School of Design.

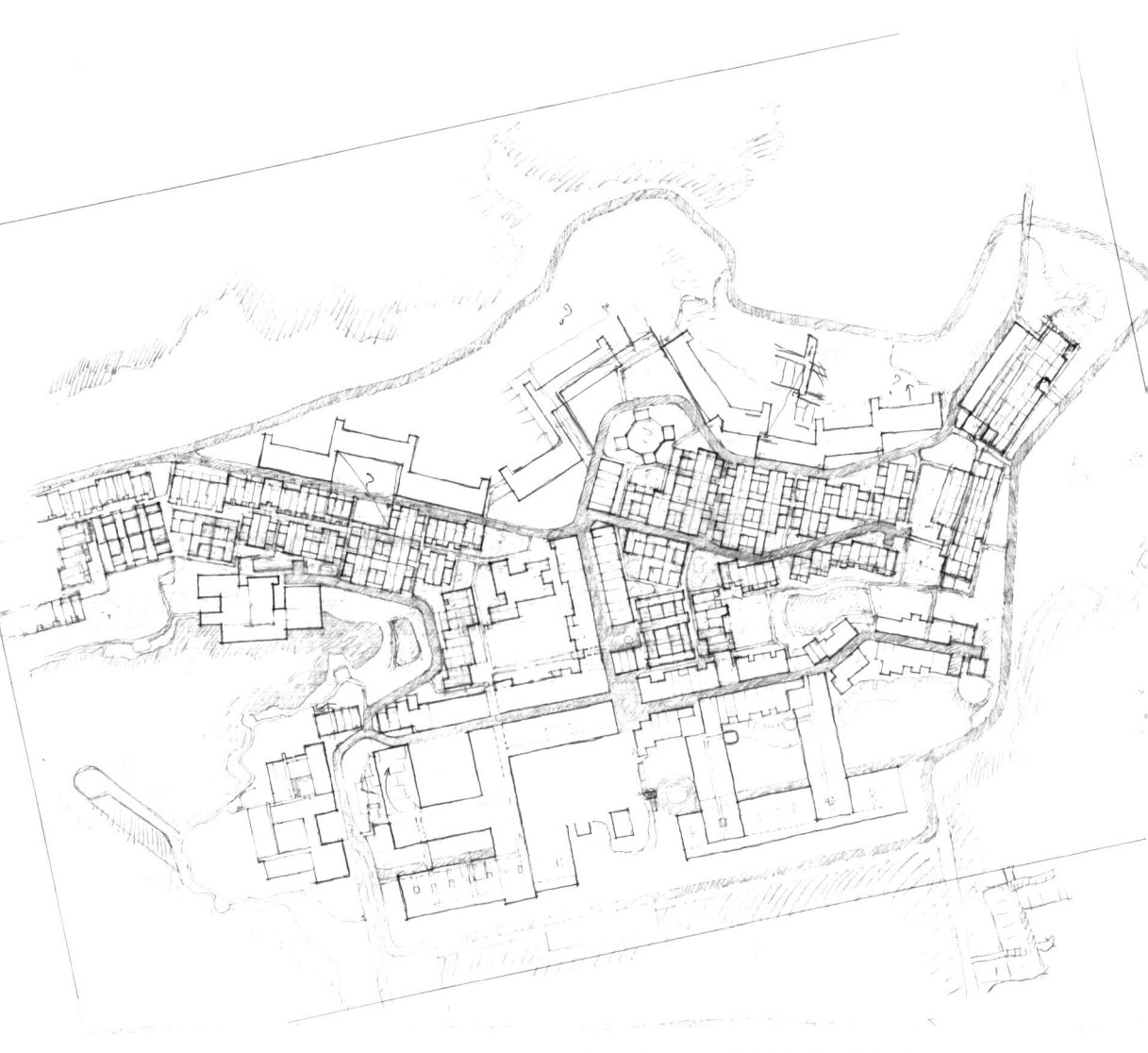

Sert, Jackson & Associates, Frioul Islands vacation village, offshore from Marseille, 1969. Sketch site plan.

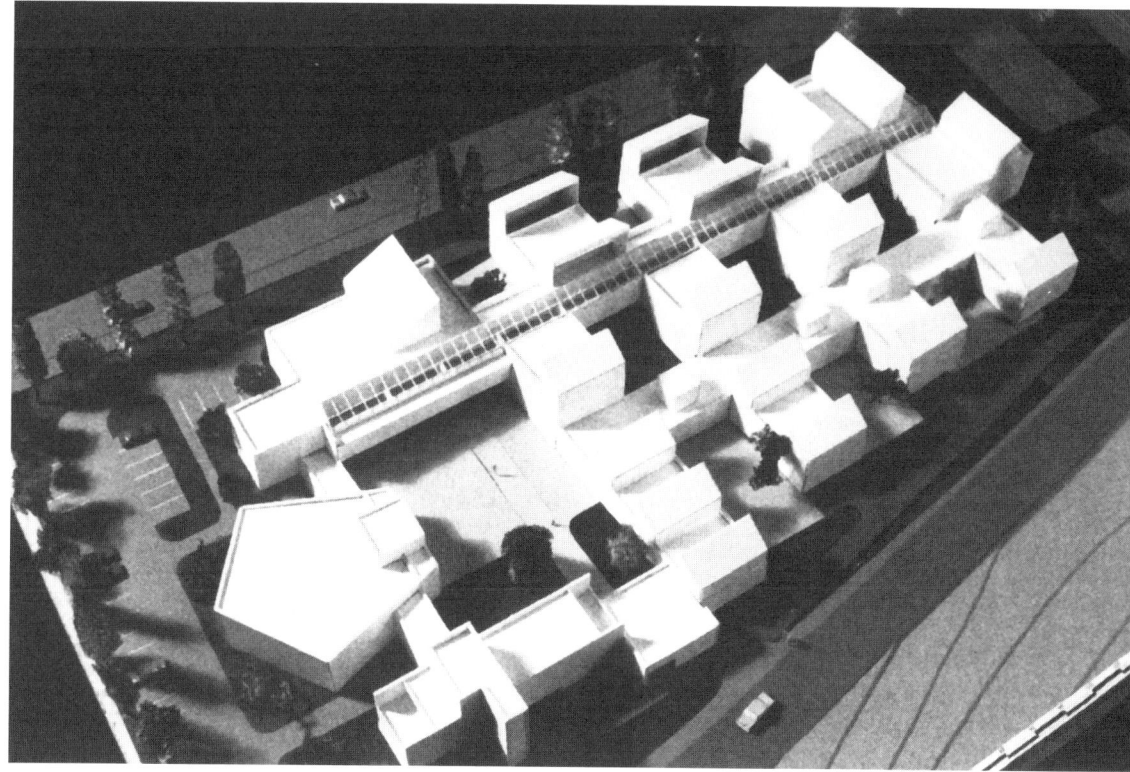

Sert, École des Beaux-Arts, Besançon, France, 1967. View of model.

- The automobile in the shrinking house.
- The parking lots in the central sectors—mass transportation the only answer.
- Sert, Jackson & Associates plan for the Frioul Islands [walkable vacation village]—how easy plans are without cars.
- The right of man to walk more freely at ground level—his feet on the ground, as against walking on concrete slabs.

There is today an increasing spirit of revolt against the life conditions in cities. People have lost the streets they once knew—streets mainly for pedestrians. "Pedestrian" has now become a derogatory term. (See Bernard Rudofsky's "Streets for People")

We are still a very young nation, and until recently we believed we had enough land to use and abuse. We invented the skyscraper but never solved its effects on the land below, at street level (see later developments in New York). World Trade Center, etc., the rootless tree....

We also decided to encourage limitless sprawl by building expressways and extending utilities that crisscross the entire country—only the great oceans stop them from going further.

Boston and San Francisco. Two cities, different from all others with a particular character and personality, are now going the way of all big cities—the same clusters of skyscrapers, same types of buildings, same congestion. The contours of hills, the shape of the sites will be hidden behind the ever-growing new additions. A new city could parallel the old—but instead of that, it destroys it. The State House on the hill, the hill itself will soon disappear.... The new expressways opened areas for development. The city need not lose its income base, all that is required is to move it to a new and appropriate location.

There is hope—maybe a last hope for our cities. The increasing revolt of the people against increasing abuse—pollution of air and water, visual pollution, noise pollution. Traffic congestion, intolerable conditions of dwellings.

Of all the challenges to the architect and the city planner today, the design of residential sectors, where houses and all the necessary services are in a planned, landscaped environment, is the greatest. This country is still very much a developing country in terms of housing—especially low-income housing. But it rates behind the Scandinavian countries, Holland, the Central European countries, England, Switzerland, etc.

The fight has just started. The much talked-about breakthrough is still far away—many barriers and many bridges have to be crossed.

15

INDUSTRIALIZATION
AN OPPORTUNITY FOR THE DESIGN
OF NEW COMMUNITIES (1974)

In the early 1970s, Sert and his firm were commissioned for urban design works in the Shah's Iran, then a repressive Western-oriented monarchy, along with many other internationally known designers such as Ian McHarg (then a partner in Wallace, McHarg, Roberts & Todd), Alvar Aalto, Georges Candilis, Richard Llewelyn-Davies, I. M. Pei, and Kenzo Tange.[1] This lecture was given in September 1974 to the Second Iranian Architects' Congress in Persepolis, an event to which such architects as Balkrishna Doshi, R. Buckminster Fuller, O. M. Ungers, and Ralph Rapson were also invited.[2] The conference and its predecessor in 1970, along with the many design projects commissioned at this time in Iran, were the result of the efforts of the Shahbanou Farah Pahlavi, an architect. One of the outcomes of the event was the effort to create a new Charter of Habitat, essentially continuing what CIAM had been attempting until its breakup in 1956.
EM

I am going to start my comments by quoting the resolutions of your previous [Iranian Architects'] Congress, four years ago:

"Above all, it is the creation of a human environment which is our primordial goal. Technology in planning and building, and the whole industrialization of the country, must be guided by that goal."

Do you really mean it? Are you prepared to live up to these statements? If so, this part of the world can work wonders, can set an example for others to follow. Let us then jointly analyze the implications and possibilities, sincerely and openly . . .

This country is in the early stages of a process of industrialization that other countries—Western Europe, the U.S., and Japan—went through many years ago. It can analyze, study, and judge what has happened in those countries, what has proved good or beneficial to man through the years and what the consequences of terrible mistakes have been. These mistakes, made more evident in recent years, have only now started to be evaluated. If continued, the consequences to the human environment could be catastrophic.

Pollution of air, water, and soil, visual pollution, and noise pollution create an unlivable environment. If we want to correct or prevent these ills, the repetition and extension of such conditions, we have to investigate their causes, the driving forces that have transformed the industrialized countries in our world.

I am especially concerned with the particular conditions of industrialization as they affect the physical habitat of man. The effects of the new means of transportation, the congestion and not the use but the abuse of the land, the economic and social conditions in communities resulting in an unnatural, dehumanized environment: all of these are affecting the lives and happiness of millions.

We have heard recently of these antihuman conditions in cities, statistics proving them are abundant, yet nothing really effective is being done. We have no great plans to correct these conditions; all that is being done in the more powerful countries is "patch-up planning."

Modern architecture, using new and advanced techniques, has produced only a relatively few good buildings. Against this, our times are witnessing the greatest urban disintegration

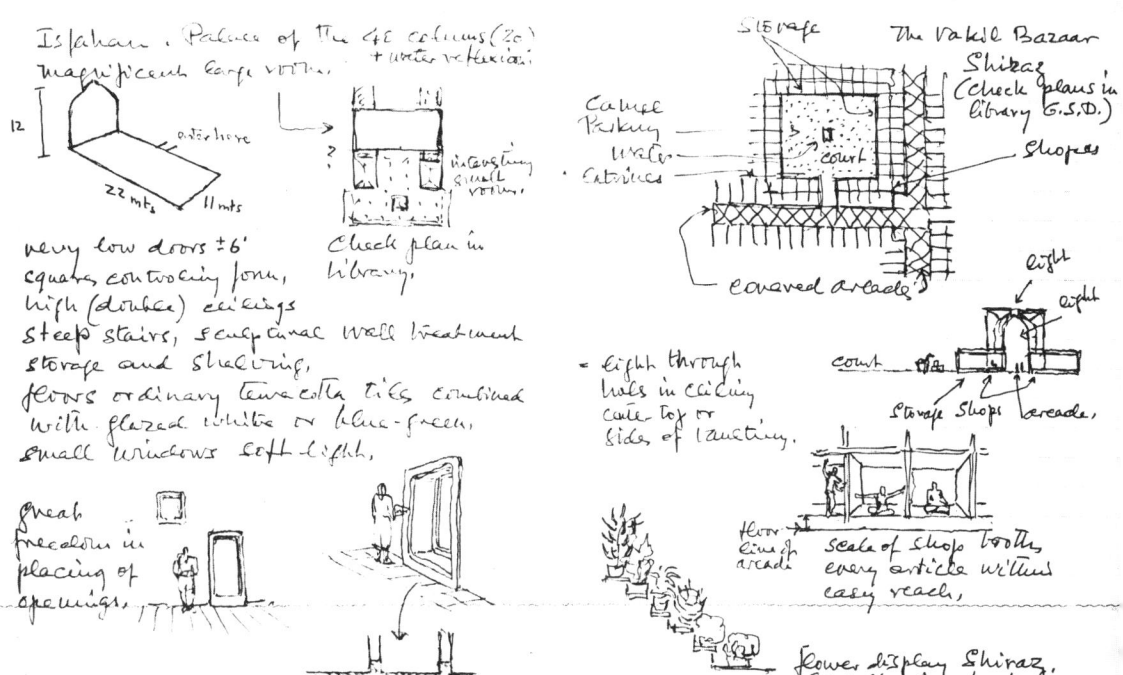

Sert, drawings from Isfahan and Shiraz, Iran, early 1970s.

the world has known: disintegration of form and scale, pollution of the environment. Living conditions in cities like Paris, London, New York, Chicago, etc., are in many ways worse today than they were at the turn of the century. This is especially true in terms of congestion, over-extension, and pollution of the regional environment.

Why do countries not put a stop to this continued environmental decay and chaos? Everybody should be aware that as long as we continue to plant the same kind of seed, the result will be the same trees. It is at the roots, in the social and economic infrastructure of our cities, that the evil lies.

Our cities are, physically, a direct result and a near-perfect expression of the systems that gave them birth. The inflated values of land, the irrational taxation, the so-called free initiatives that lack wide vision and cater only for immediate gains and rapid returns on investments: these are the causes.

I saw recently, on my television screen in Cambridge, some views of Alexandria in Egypt. A city with a noble past, once a world center of learning, it looked like another miserable copy of Miami Beach. And it is the same with the once beautiful Copacabana in Rio. Hong Kong increasingly resembles Detroit, while San Francisco, once a promise, will soon look like any other city. The shape of the site, the land and the hills, disappears in the mass of disorderly, unscaled, inhuman building.

When Le Corbusier built his Unite d'Habitation in Marseilles, right after the last world war, the whole of France attacked him. He called it Unite de Grandeur Conforme, which sounded rather pompous or ridiculous. But he was right, and you can see it if you go to that city now. Le Corbusier's building is large but still very human in scale; the later development masks the hills and landscape. Le Corbusier's building is set in the landscape; the new ones are set against it.

We have arrived at a moment when technically and economically—not socially, not humanly—there are no limits to size, and we can violate the scale of the site and the environment at will. But everything that is economically feasible (the feasibility studies are one-sided) becomes a possible reality, and so monsters are born. Outstanding examples are the ever higher and larger office buildings in the centers of cities, the so-called CBDS (central business districts), the housing developments with too many people crowded into buildings that are much too high, all the open land used for parking and blacktopped. This is even more visible in resort areas (like the Mediterranean and the Caribbean islands), where hotels are of a size resulting from financial and not human calculations. These sites have what amounts to a continuous concrete wall or barrier cutting the water front off from the interior.

There is enough criticism, but little action in our day. I would now like to make a few constructive proposals, in the hope (I have always been an optimist) that they may be of help to your country, which is now starting a process of industrialization that will mean profound changes in the way of life of its inhabitants.

I have had a long and varied experience in the fields of design, as they affect architecture regarded as part of the bigger complex of the city; experience starting in Europe in the changing years of the twenties, then continued in fifteen years of planning work in South America (from my New York office), and later on in my sixteen years in Harvard University—at the Graduate School of Design—and now in private practice. And I have learned the following:

← FAST → | → SLOW ← | ← FAST →

FAST ← | FAST – SLOW – STOP | → FAST

The urban-architectural elements
The Ford Foundation building – offices could open on green malls (Cristal Palace)
- The L.C. building in Algiers – proto-mega-structure
- The terminal concourse – Grand Central – Penn Station +
- The Rome terminal, – Bus Terminal N.Y.
- Rock. Center – Place Bonaventure – Habitat – Scarborough Coll. Holyoke arcade – Pedestrian tours...

Sert, drawing of speeds of urban perception, with his list of important urban projects in the West.

Firstly, that a human environment conducive to the "pursuit of happiness" cannot be dominated or controlled by financial feasibility alone. Livability, the enjoyment of life and with it the preservation and improvement of site conditions—topography, sunshine, shade, trees, water—are also unconditionally essential parts of our lives.

Secondly, that a balance between open and built-up land has to be established in view of human requirements. Social conditions and human relationships are part of the required balance, for surely people are brought together to benefit from that very experience of being together.

Thirdly, the dispersion encouraged by the automobile is anti-communal and anti-urban. No television screen can replace the handshake. Community life, even if the communities of today are very different from those of tomorrow, is not replaceable by remote-control systems and never will be.

The great challenge of our time, the great opportunity for industrializing countries, is to develop balanced, harmonious communities which will be the expression of better ways of life for the people as a whole. In this country you have the possibility and the financial resources not only to improve your existing cities and guide and control their development, but to establish and develop new, balanced communities, towns, and cities or clusters and constellations of communities, wherever needed.

The key to the new communities is balance, by which I mean the proper size or scale and relationships of all parts, and the proper closeness and compactness that the urban environment requires, without overcrowding, without destruction of the best elements of the nature-made site.

The community must be measured by the pedestrian, must be a place where it is enjoyable to walk in porticoed streets, arcades, small parks, pedestrian streets, helped by slow means of public transport. I say "slow" because speed is meaningless when distances are short, and low speeds can mix properly with pedestrians in compact communities. For centuries the horse-drawn carriage mixed with pedestrians without great complications. Slow means of mechanical transport, such as minibuses or moving sidewalks, can be sufficient in a compact community center. All automobiles could then be banned from the more central areas and remain in a well-planned and publicly controlled peripheral garage system.

Parking facilities proportionate to the size of community should be managed by a parking authority and linked directly to the expressway system. Public transport would then extend from the parking structures to the cores or nuclei of the community. Depending on the size of the community, the public transport facilities would consist of simple bus lines, moving sidewalks, etc.

The planned and limited densities of population, which can be high or medium at the core of the compact community—250-400 to the acre, for instance, in a compact plan, would help to keep distances short, bring people together and encourage personal contacts. Pedestrian movements, using a system of porticoed streets or arcades (some air-conditioned), could make walking a pleasure. Simple mechanical systems or devices could assist older people and those carrying parcels or children. The dangers, noises, and pollution of traffic as we know it today would be eliminated. (The moving sidewalks have already found wide application in airports.)

I am not talking of a utopian fantasy, of some remote future, but of something that can be immediately transformed into reality, and at reasonable cost. Certain lines of main movement

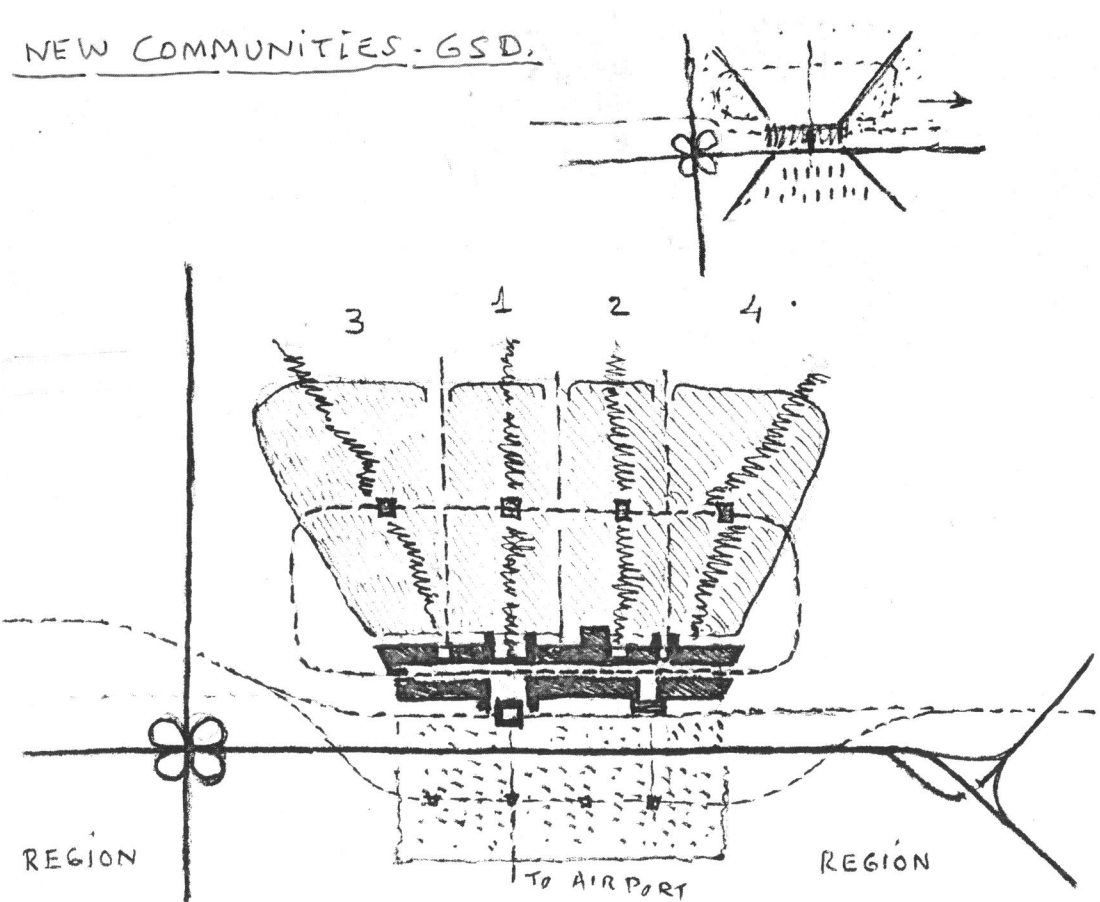

Sert, sketch diagram for "New Communities," undated, circa 1968.

Sert, Jackson & Associates, Roosevelt Island mixed-use housing for the New York State Urban Development Corporation, 1970–75. Aerial view.

and their architectural expression would result in linear backbone developments that would give the community a visual expression, a definite shape—as it would be composed and seen from the air—of main movement lines with a strong, three-dimensional expression and infill areas, still compact but of medium densities. The whole would be strangely reminiscent of the old communities in your country and other countries in this part of the world. In infill areas, patio or courtyard houses would be appropriate, as they provide privacy, controlled views, and garden areas easy to maintain. Trees will predominate in height over buildings and fences, so that streets can be harmonious, quiet, and unpretentious, and everybody can build anything he likes behind his fence.

The plans for such balanced, compact communities economize on utility extensions, roads, sidewalks, and park areas—all easy to design but costly to build and maintain. We have seen too many plans that look very good on paper, but in which green areas and strips become, in reality, unkempt dustbowls where refuse collects, as nobody is interested in their upkeep and the municipality cannot, or will not, maintain them in proper shape. In our work for Latin American cities, new and old, we soon came to the conclusion that public areas should be kept to a controllable size and that all other open land should become part of the houses or buildings making direct use of it.

What I am trying to describe is something that I have designed and measured very carefully for many cities and over many years. I have taken into consideration the cost factors, the ways of living of the people involved, and the fact that we are facing a transitional period. Some of the elements that could develop in such communities I have tried, whenever possible, to experiment within my work. I have worked especially on housing, and preferentially on publicly subsidized housing, in recent years.

Like all housing in central areas of American cities (this also applies to Western Europe), the program requires too many units on the site "to offset land costs and taxes." We have tried to do our best with the given restraints and limitations. We have worked from the inside outwards; that is to say, from the best possible unit plans to their clusters and to the circulation links with the public spaces, open or given up to community facilities. For housing is more than houses; it is a part—and an expression—of a way of living.

Through years of work we have acquired a sense of the structure and measure of a community that would set an example by providing a better and more human way of living. We are aware that what is being done today (with the exception of a few scattered examples, all incomplete) is only making conditions in our cities increasingly worse, especially as these affect people, their lives and their health and happiness.

> I have two suggestions to make:
> 1. The immediate building of one or more model new communities, based on radically new and different premises and programs.
> 2. The preparation of teams of architect-planners to work with economists, geographers (ecologists), sociologists, educators, health specialists, and engineers (specializing in transport, traffic, etc.) in order to properly to undertake the formidable task we face in planning for the immediate future.

A "Watergate" of those responsible for the deteriorating conditions in our cities is long overdue. You cannot ask technicians or professionals to correct the evils of our cities without exposing the causes of these evils. I recommend that groups of architectural planning schools all over the world unite to develop programs to investigate the causes that have produced, and are producing, the urban catastrophe of our time. They could then proceed to denounce those causes and formulate a charter for new communities and the correction of conditions in existing ones.

We must have a Charter of Urban Rights—just as we have a Charter of Human Rights—to be endorsed by international associations such as the U.N. and UNESCO, as well as by the countries wanting to join.

As for the schools of environmental studies, architecture, landscape architecture, and city and regional planning, even the best of them are conformist in their approach today. They try to do the best they can and take it for granted that existing conditions are unchangeable, that the forces that shape our environment, though manmade, cannot be altered or redirected, that legislation and established principles that have been found to work against human interests, health, and happiness cannot be changed. This is the attitude of a timid generation. New priorities will have to be established, a different set of values accepted.

For this purpose I suggest that in the designing of new communities, or the redesigning of existing ones, we apply the proposed Charter of Urban Rights as a guiding element. This is not in any way a constraint or limitation of technical or design possibilities. All the Charter of Urban Rights would do would be similar to what the Charter of Human Rights does: allows greater freedom and works with people to help them develop their full potential. The constraints or limitations are what we have today, as we are conditioned by the restraints imposed by "developers" guided by so-called "realistic conditions."

In synthesis, I would recommend that this country be the first in the world to build a really new community as an experiment. In your industrialization process, you will be trying many experiments: mock-ups of cars, planes, machines of all types—all this is part of the process. I suggest that you apply the same criteria to your new experimental community. You will try prefabrication methods, and you can benefit from what has been initiated in different countries; and the same criteria will apply to the whole infrastructure of the community: utilities, roads, etc. As the new community takes shape, it will become a teaching experiment. Your new programs in your renovated schools will also be experimenting on how to move forward from this initial experiment.

A new horizon can be wide open for your people. You may be the first country where industrialization builds, on a beautiful architectural past, the most promising visual picture of a better future; where nature, people, and machines will come together and contribute to a harmonious environment.

16
BALANCE IN THE HUMAN HABITAT (1977)

This is the text of a talk that Sert delivered at the University of Tennessee on November 1, 1977, a few years before his death in 1983. It explains the ideas behind the *Habitat Bill of Rights* (Tehran: Hamdami Foundation, 1976), presented by the government of the Shah's Iran to the U.N. Conference on Human Settlements in Vancouver in June 1976. The *Habitat Bill of Rights* was a direct outcome of the 1974 Persepolis Congress, which had included Sert, as he mentions here. Sert also sums up the main ideas behind his work in two built projects, the Peabody Terrace Married Student Housing for Harvard (1961) and the mixed-use housing complexes that his firm designed for the New York State Urban Development Corporation on Roosevelt Island in New York City and in nearby Yonkers (1970).

EM

I am happy to be here in Knoxville to deliver the Robert Church Memorial Lecture at this university.

I am looking forward to visiting the university and this part of the country, which I have heard much about but never visited before. Practically every architect in Europe had heard about the Tennessee Valley Authority project and, after the last Great War, all new arrivals in New York wanted to visit this part of the land, which was considered an outstanding example of good planning at that time. I will have many questions to ask some of you, but I will leave these for our informal meetings tomorrow.

Tonight I will talk to you about a matter I have long been concerned with—housing as part of the urban environment. I will deal only with high- and medium-density low-income housing, as it contributes to an urban way of life, as part of a community, in residential areas of large cities.

In spite of the declining conditions of living in such cities, more and more people in every country are moving to the urban areas, disrupting the balance once existing between urban and rural populations.

We are all concerned with the problems posed by the explosive growth of world population, but we are doing practically nothing for a better and more rational distribution, as this growth is paralleled by a chaotic expansion of our larger cities.

People do not only come to cities in search of work; they come to live better. They come to find better living conditions, education, health care, better homes, entertainment, and especially greater opportunities for meeting other people.

Many, like their forefathers, had lived in small, remote communities, devoid of elementary services and amenities, where they were often exploited. They come to the cities to find a new and better way of life. Instead, they are obliged to live in the worst conditions, far worse in most respects than those they left behind. They become the low-paid labor supply, and exploitation continues.

I had opportunities to see such conditions in South America during twelve years of work in projects for those countries.

I visited the *favelas* in Rio de Janeiro and the *barriadas* in Lima, Peru. We developed studies for compact, low-rise residential districts in the late forties' and early fifties'. In 1947 we worked on the plan for the city of Chimbote in Peru, developing new patterns using patio houses, the first plan of its kind.

When living in New York, I worked with the Citizens Housing Council, then making a critical study of the gloomy standardized public housing plans of the 1930s.

My work in housing started in Europe, before my arrival in this country in 1939. My thoughts on housing and urban planning in those years (while working with the International Congresses for Modern Architecture, known as CIAM) were summarized in *Can Our Cities Survive?* published in 1942 by Harvard University Press.

I continued exploring this subject while teaching in the masters' class at the Graduate School of Design at Harvard. Twelve years ago, together with my partners and associates, we were able to test these ideas in the [Peabody Terrace] Married Student Housing built for Harvard University, and, recently, in our work for the Urban Development Corporation in New York.

In September 1974, I was invited to the Second Iranian International Congress of Architects in Persepolis. This Congress was convened by the Ministry of Housing and Urban Development of that country.

4 The pedestrian precinct should include suitable mixed land uses so as to provide local enterprise and employment.

Pedestrian Precinct Recommendations

Suitable uses may consist of local retail outlets, restaurants and cafes, commercial entertainment and recreation, professional and commercial offices, research and development activities, including clean light industrial uses, repair and storage services and the like.

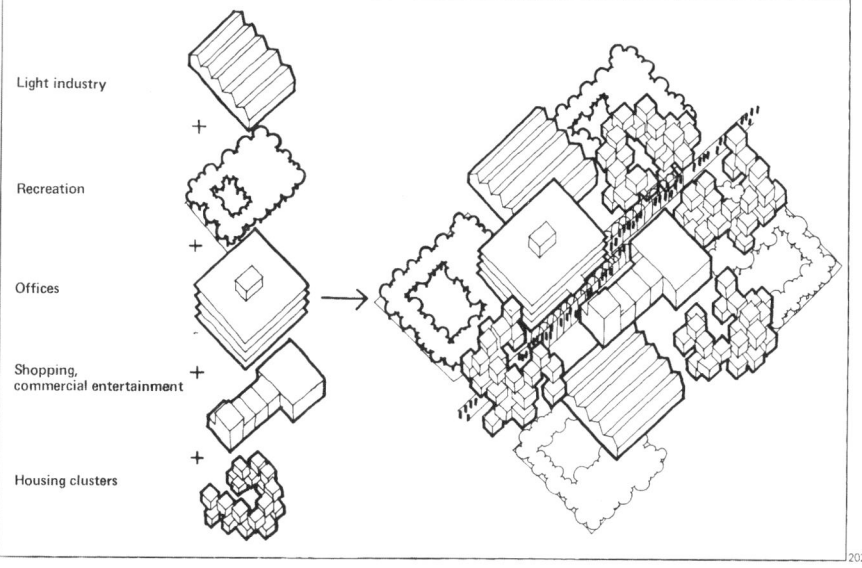

202 The potential of land use development.

Three-dimensional mixed-use pedestrian precinct land-use recommendations, from *Habitat Bill of Rights* (Tehran: Hamdami Foundation, 1976).

Sert, Jackson & Associates, Peabody Terrace Married Student Housing, Harvard University, Cambridge, Massachusetts, 1961–63.

Fortunately, it was a rather small gathering—about seventy-five people—more or less the numbers that came to our CIAM Congresses. This permitted us to communicate and to formulate resolutions. There were people from many different countries: the U.S., the People's Republic of China, the U.S.S.R., Western Europe, India, the Near East.

It was curious to note that many of the subjects discussed at the CIAM gatherings were still controversial, [even] after the many years that had elapsed.

The Persepolis Congress adopted the following resolution:
Through research studies, a code of human habitat should be developed with such procedures and strategies necessary to the achievement of principles essential to the creation of a wholesome, balanced, and equitable habitat. This code should be so prepared that it may form a working tool suitable for use by all the decision makers involved in the shaping of the human habitat in time and place.

PEDESTRIAN PRECINCT 3
150 TO 1500 UNITS

MEASURE / SCALE	¼ MILE (400 M) WALKING RADIUS SERVICES: ELEM. SCHOOL, SHOPS AMENITIES: RECREATION, WATER PLAY, SHARED WORKSHOP, STUDIO
IDENTITY	IDENTIFIED WITH SCHOOL UNIQUENESS DUE TO LANDMARKS HARMONIOUS VARIETY OF BLDG. TYPES
TERRITORIALITY	CLEAR BOUNDARIES & ENTRY ASSIGN UPKEEP OF COMMON SPACES OVERLOOK PUBLIC SPACES & ENTRIES
RELATION TO NATURE	PROVIDE BODY OF WATER, CONSERVATION STANDARDS FOR LANDSCAPING e.g. 1 CAR = 1 TREE. DIFFERENTIATE PRECINCTS THRU PLANTING
ACCESS / MOVEMENT	INTEGRATE SLOW CARS & PROMENADE MINIMUM SETBACK FROM ROADS ACTIVATE GROUND LEVEL
ANIMATION	FORMAL & INFORMAL MEETING PLACES EXPRESS MOVEMENT NETWORK; PEDES. EXPRESS VARIETY OF HOUSING TYPES
GROWTH / FLEX	RESERVE LAND OVERLAPPING ZONES OF SERVICE FUTURE GARAGES; INTERSECTIONS

Sert, guidelines for pedestrian precincts, from *Balanced Habitat* (unpublished), 1977.

As a means to test and implement the above code, several prototype communities are recommended to be built and continuously evaluated. The evaluation methodology and process may be undertaken by a task force of international reputation in many different fields. The objective would be to achieve compact and balanced communities.

An international committee was formed to undertake this preliminary study; the members of this committee are Nader Ardalan (Iran), Georges Candilis (France), Balkrishna Doshi (India), Georges Kondracki (United Nations), Moshe Safdie (Canada), and Josep Lluís Sert (U.S.), chairman.

The committee met in New York, Tehran, Paris, Cambridge, and Montreal. The tentative code document, called the Habitat Bill of Rights, was submitted in preliminary draft shape by the Iranian Ministry of Housing and Urban Development at the United Nations Conference on Human Settlements in Vancouver, held in June 1976.

We had done valuable research in Cambridge and Montreal. We had had the assistance and advice of several specialists (Professor William Doebele from Harvard University, Jaqueline Tyrwhitt of *Ekistics* in Athens, Professor Edward Tsoi of Harvard University).

The document is still being completed for publication.

The committee was united in overcoming divergences. The work and discussions were, for me, reminiscent of the best times of the CIAM.

The origins of such an effort can actually be traced back to the last CIAM meetings, and especially to Le Corbusier, who had suggested that the Congress draft a Charte de l'Habitat in 1956.

Corbu's outstanding faith in the possibility of developing a habitat worthy of our times and our culture remained a guiding force until the Congresses were terminated in 1956. The project was never carried through.

The task of the committee, as defined by the above-mentioned resolution, limits the study to residential areas or sectors of cities. We found existing codes in different nations mainly concerned with quantitative factors, ignoring qualitative elements, which have been our main concern. Our study deals with housing related to all other factors that compose the urban residential habitat, such as all supporting services and amenities. How to attain the quality of urban living, appropriate densities, links to other urban sectors are the roots of the problem.

Densities have been a major consideration. It is evident that technology at the service of certain interests has resulted in extremist attitudes in planning, and this country offers too many examples of this type. We find, on one hand, vast suburban areas with overextended utilities, where every movement needs the use of the automobile. The result is low densities with dispersion, destruction of the natural sites, overextension of roads and utilities, increase in costs of the infrastructure and its maintenance. (See "The Costs of Sprawl," available from the U.S. Department of Housing and Urban Development.)

The opposite extreme occurs in central areas. There, highrise buildings break all ceilings. Congestion of people and cars reaches maximum figures. Land is not only intensively used, it is abused. Community life there, like in suburban sprawl, is impossible to organize.

But there is a range of densities that makes community life possible, both in physical and economic terms. Within these densities, balanced compact communities can be organized. Our Habitat Bill of Rights has carefully considered these conditions. Balance implies a correct relationship of all parts to the whole:

- Balance between the communal and the private
- Balance between dwellings, supporting services and amenities
- Balance between people and automobiles, or families and "wheels"
- Balance between areas occupied by buildings and open areas, people and trees
- Balance between passive and active recreation (quiet and noise)
- Balance between the nature given and the man-made elements
- Balance between low walk-up buildings and higher ones using elevators—it should not be high vs. low, but the balanced combination of high and low
- Balance between new technology and older traditional methods—giving a feeling of cultural continuity, when appropriate

The ultimate aim is the resulting balanced and harmonious way of life; quality of living is the real goal, as part of the "pursuit of happiness."

This bill of rights is concerned with the rights of people living in communities, towns or cities, old or new. Its contents are limited to residential areas. It deals with:

- Dwellings
- Clusters, or groups of dwellings
- Pedestrian precinct
- Urban community
- Housing in developing countries

It does not pretend to be all inclusive; it is, rather, a chapter of a much more extensive study that would relate to habitat on a national and regional scale.

This Habitat Bill of Rights tries to define the qualitative issues connected with the design of houses and their groupings into new communities (or existing ones) as a supplement to other codes and regulations which have attempted to define only quantitative issues related to building. In our concern with qualitative factors, we find that many of them do not relate to cost and are applicable to the most needy developing countries. Such are: identity, territoriality, consideration of climate conditions, good views, preservation of natural conditions, a sense of entrance, correct proportions and scale, animation, use of color, etc. Others do not relate to cost either, but to abuses committed in the most developed countries (the overdeveloped ones) to obtain greater profits that tend to lower the quality of life and prevent the balanced development that should be our goal.

Technology, if guided toward the balanced development, can be of great help. Unfortunately, it is generally used to lower costs and increase benefits to developers, rather than improve the quality of life that should be the main goal of our efforts.

It would take much more time than I dispose of here today to outline this Habitat Bill of Rights as the committee in charge of that work, which lasted two years, has formulated it. For me, this team work has added to the experiences of the last five years, and it is of these that I will talk to you now.

Together with my partners, associates, and all the design group in my office, we have been involved in several housing projects, three of which I will now show you and comment on.

The first project is the Married Student Housing complex built for Harvard University twelve years ago. This project is closely related to the two New York schemes which will follow in this presentation.

Peabody Terrace is composed of five hundred units on a six-acre site facing the Charles River. It is basically a community of a revolving population of young families coming from many different countries, but approximately of the same age bracket. It had to fit the existing environment of the older Harvard student houses along the Charles River, which are equivalent in height to five to seven stories of the new types. On the other side, it had to relate to ordinary Cambridge one-family frame houses and the Martin Luther King public school on Putnam Avenue, designed by us.

These are the basic design characteristics of the project:

a) the adoption throughout of a basic cluster of units that feeds off a single loaded corridor, one floor up and one down. This disposition divides all heights, horizontally, in three-floor modules. Expression of the walk-up measure that appears in the lower blocks gives a scale within a scale to the higher ones.

b) the adoption of the single-loaded corridor in preference to the double-loaded one. The double-loaded types, if we exclude duplex-type apartments (which were too costly for the kind of housing required), generally result in kitchens with no direct views or light and having to use mechanical ventilation—cave-like kitchens. Otherwise, too much frontage is required. To sell the single-loaded corridors we baptized them "triple-loaded," because they serve three floors. The single-loaded corridors with continuous glazing economize energy and make movements from elevators to entrances of apartments more agreeable (livability factor) because they have views to the outside. They also provide more security, because they can be observed from the outside. Area-wise, these corridors represent a minimum given to circulation when divided by three.

c) This single-loaded corridor, three-floor cluster grouping provides 66 percent of the apartments with through-ventilation and double exposure—sunrise to sunset—which means an awareness of the twenty-four-hour cycle of the sun that governs and measures our daily existence. Kitchens have wide views and are an extension of the living room that can, at will, be united or separated.

Somebody asked us, "How is it that the apartments in the subsidized housing are better than the more expensive ones?" My answer: it is you that set the rules, and wealthier people seem to have more prejudices—they cannot walk one floor up or down, so they cannot have through-views. Our subsidized apartments have even better views than the expensive penthouses in Sutton Place across the river—too bad!

Sert, Jackson & Associates, Riverview apartment complex, Yonkers, New York, 1973-74.

The up- or down-going stairs are an additional visual element, enlarging and providing animation to the living space. These layouts provide sun to all apartments in the buildings, which have double-orientation—north/south, east/west, or intermediate.

The single-loaded corridor types also are easier to combine and turn angles without loss of floor space. The basic clusters of six apartments in Peabody Terrace or three apartments in the New York projects permit a variety of steps in the different buildings. With the systems, it is easy to develop well-defined community spaces (quadrangles) that can be enclosed and given to the exclusive use of the abutting apartments, offering greater protection. Stepped-down apartment blocks allow for lower groups on sides where sun should penetrate or views should be opened. The system, in terms of urban design, provides the necessary variety and flexibility.

The accessibility of all roofs by families is important. Terraces on steps are convenient for tot lots and storage of toys for children, sunbathing facilities, and showers. This was allowed in Cambridge but forbidden in New York, in spite of their beautiful views on the East River. The excuse given was "dangerous, encouraging suicides and drug peddling."

Architectural expression: following the principles we apply to all buildings, the exterior treatments express interior uses and circulation spaces (lines of movement). Community living areas in apartments are distinguishable as projecting volumes with larger windows in the New York projects, where balconies were not permitted. In Peabody Terrace, we have balconies with sun-protection devices. Corridors are emphasized, with continuous strip windows emphasizing movements and accesses to apartments.

Elevator towers, stairs, and fire escapes are particularly accentuated in the New York projects, following tradition in that city, although their treatment is totally different from the usual one. They are concrete shafts that also help the rigidity of the slabs.

Structure is not emphasized. The Urban Development Corporation asked us to study a variety of structural possibilities. They first considered structures and outside perimeter walls as prefabricated in a nearby plant (Tracoba Systems) to be transported by barges to the island. Later, other systems were considered, also ordinary flat slabs. Finally, Building Systems, Inc., got the job. They used bearing walls and slabs cast in situ with special table forms for slabs and metal forms for walls. Walls were not prefabricated, and we were asked to use brick for the outer skin of the buildings—8 foot × 8 foot pieces with vertical grooves were selected. In Cambridge, we were allowed to use precast panels, which proved much faster to assemble. The houses built by John Johansen across the Main Street made use of extruded cement asbestos panels. But UDC did not want further experiments.

Last but not least in all these projects, like in other office work, we have made use of proportion controls: squares and golden means rectangles appear frequently, defining volumes, fenestration, and voids between buildings. Also, we have tried very hard within our cost limitations to enliven the total views by textures and color accents. Many ideas were never carried out. We lost many battles, but won a few!

The Urban Development Corporation and Ed Logue encouraged and accepted "new design" ideas. And the work done by their group, in which we had many friends, has an outstanding record of better housing in New York State, if compared to what had been done previously by other agencies. It was, in some ways, too good to last, and unfortunately [the lack of] government support and the negative attitude in Washington during the Nixon administration toward housing in general and public housing in particular made the UDC close up shop. But the results are there to speak for their good intentions and to prove that, if proper priorities are given to improving the urban habitat, this country can, and one day will, find new ways to comply with that "pursuit of happiness" as it affects the environment. *It will only have taken two hundred years!*

There is a long road and many difficulties to overcome to see some examples of better habitats materialize. Which will be the first country to produce examples of what we know can and will one day be done?

The harmonious, balanced community is an easy possibility compared with extraterrestrial exploration; the obstacles, mainly economic, will first have to be removed. They are man-made and, as John F. Kennedy said, "it only takes men to remove them." *Human rights are accepted by the majority of nations as part of their basic legislation.* The application of similar principles referring to the rights of urban dwellers, to the urban habitat, may be a reality soon.

ACKNOWLEDGMENTS

This book would not have appeared without the strong and continuing support of Melissa Vaughn, senior editor at the Harvard Graduate School of Design, and of Michelle Komie, former senior editor for art and architecture at Yale University Press. Thanks also to Katherine Boller and Heidi Downey at Yale for carrying this project through to completion, and to Jena Sher for a compelling book design. Many thanks also to Mary Daniels, former acting director of the Frances Loeb Library and for many years the special collections archivist at GSD, and her successor Inés Zalduendo. Their assistance in finding the archival texts and many of the illustrations included here was invaluable, as were their many years of sound advice. I am also grateful to GSD Dean Mohsen Mostafavi for his support for this project and for writing the foreword. Bruno Maurer, archivist at the CIAM Archives, ETH Zurich, was also very helpful in assisting my research on CIAM for this and other projects. I would also like to thank Mindy Carney for making the transcription of the original typed documents from the Sert archive.

The following other scholars have been especially helpful in the development of this project: Hashim Sarkis, Aga Khan Chair of Landscape Architecture and Urbanism in Muslim Societies, Harvard GSD; Josep Rovira, professor at the Escola Tècnica Superior d'Arquitectura de Barcelona (UPC), and Jaume Freixa, Barcelona; Eduard F. Sekler, Osgood Hooker Professor of Visual Art, Emeritus, Harvard GSD; Jean Louis Cohen, Sheldon H. Solow Professor at the Institute of Fine Arts, New York University; Kenneth Frampton, Ware Chair of Architecture, Emeritus, Columbia University; Mardges Bacon, Matthews Distinguished University Professor, Emeritus, Northeastern University; Sharif Kahatt, associate professor, Pontifica Universidad Católica del Perú in Lima; Carlos Eduardo Hernández Rodríguez, Leon Dario Espinosa Restrepo, and Marcela Isabel Angel Samper in Bogotá, Colombia; Patricia Schnitter Castellanos in Medellín, Colombia; Carlos Brillembourg, Columbia University; Timothy Hyde, MIT; Ivan Rupnik, Zagreb, Croatia, and Northeastern University; Laurent Stalder, ETH Zurich; Fumihiko Maki, Tokyo; Ben Weese, Chicago; and Robert Campbell. These conversations about Sert have been invaluable.

My scholarly work in this book, as in many of my previous books, has also benefited from the continuing support and collegiality of the faculty and staff of the Sam Fox School of Design and Visual Arts at Washington University in St. Louis. I would particularly like to thank Dean Carmon Colangelo, Dean Bruce Lindsey, and librarian Rina Vecchiola and her staff at the Washington University Art and Architecture Library, as well as Washington University Deans Emeritus Cynthia Weese and Constantine Michaelides.

Thanks also as always to my wife, Devora Tulcensky, and to my daughters, Sophia and Anna, for their patience during the long process of assembling this book.

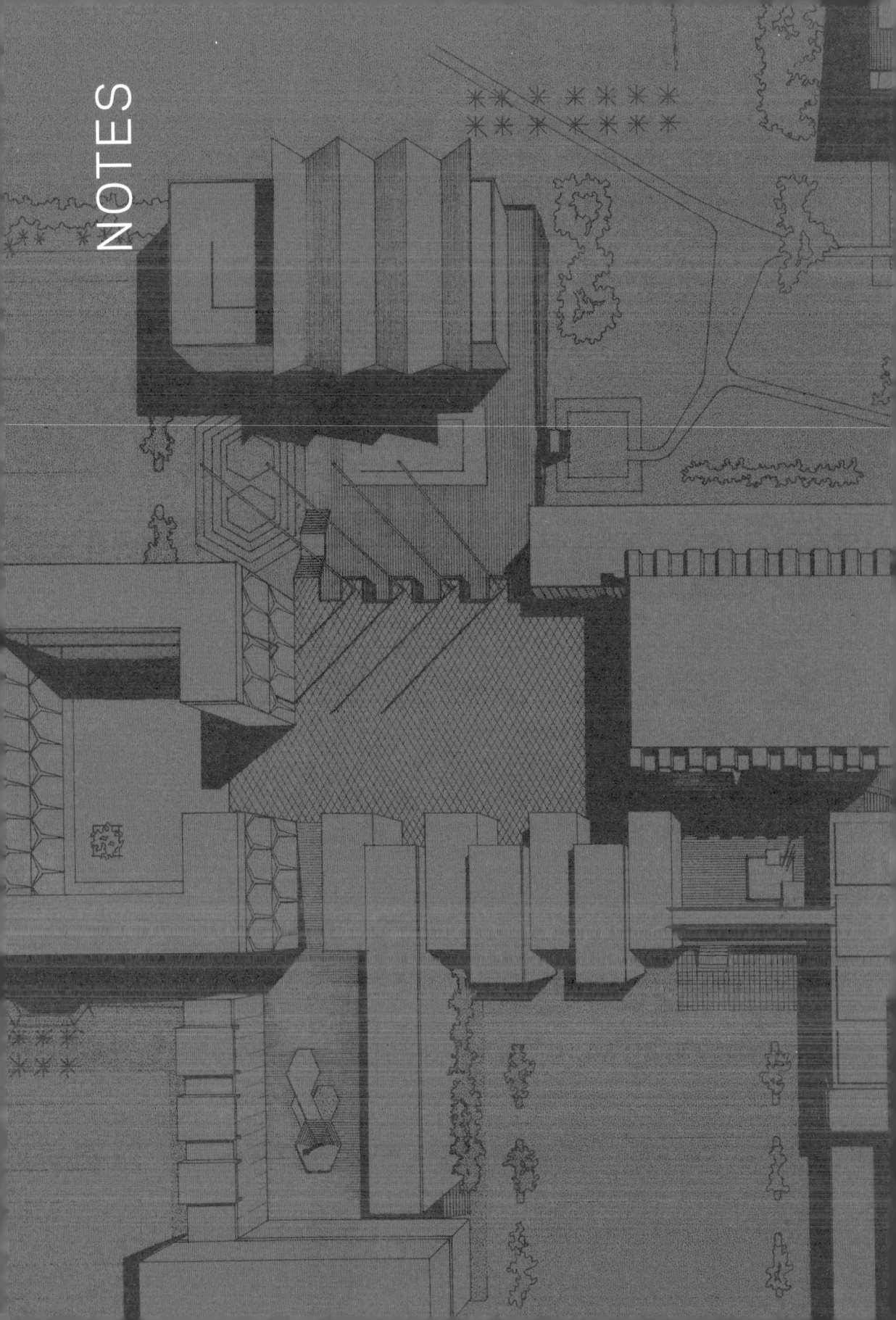

NOTES

INTRODUCTION

1   The first Sert monograph is Knud Bastlund, *José Luis Sert: Architecture, City Planning, Urban Design* (London: Thames and Hudson, 1967), prepared by a former Danish associate at Sert, Jackson & Associates. More recent works on Sert's career include Jaume Freixa, *Josep Lluís Sert* (Barcelona: Gili, 1992); Josep Rovira, *José Luis Sert, 1901–1983* (Milan: Electa, 2000); Josep M. Rovira, ed., *Sert, 1928-1979* (Barcelona: Miro Foundation, n.d.); Eric Mumford, *Defining Urban Design: CIAM Architects and the Formation of a Discipline, 1937-69* (New Haven: Yale University Press, 2009); Eric Mumford and Hashim Sarkis, eds., *Josep Lluís Sert: The Architect of Urban Design* (New Haven: Yale University Press, 2008); Antonio Pizza, "Politics and Architecture," in Antonio Pizza and Josep Rovira, eds., *GATCPAC: Una nueva arquitectura para una nueva ciudad* [A new architecture for a new city] (Barcelona, 2006), 96-125.

2   Some of these ideas are also evident in the limited collections of Sert's published writings in English, which include the essays in Bastlund, *José Luis Sert*, and those in Jaume Freixa, *Josep Lluís Sert* (Barcelona: Santa and Cole, 2005).

3   See Mumford, *Defining Urban Design*, for a detailed account of Sert's role in the formation of this field.

4   Joseph Hudnut, "Minority Report of the Harvard Committee on Regional Planning," September 10, 1940 (Harvard University Archives, GSD Papers, UAV 322.138 1940).

5   Jill Pearlman, *Inventing American Modernism: Joseph Hudnut, Walter Gropius, and the Bauhaus Legacy at Harvard* (Charlottesville: University of Virginia Press, 2007).

6   Not included here but accessible elsewhere are the proceedings of this First Harvard Urban Conference, originally published as "Urban Design," *Progressive Architecture* 37 (August 1956): 97-111, and republished in part in *Harvard Design Magazine* 24 (Spring/Summer 2006): 4-9, and in Alex Krieger and Williams S. Saunders, eds., *Urban Design* (Minneapolis: University of Minnesota Press, 2009).

7   Charles Abrams, remarks at the First Harvard Urban Design Conference, "Urban Design," 100-101.

8   This approach was developed at the Fourth CIAM Congress in 1933 and codified by Le Corbusier in his *La Charte d'Athènes* (Paris: Plon, 1943). On Team 10, see Max Risselada and Dirk van den Heuvel, *Team 10, 1953-81: In Search of a Utopia of the Present* (Rotterdam: NAi, 2003).

9   See Mumford, *Defining Urban Design*, 88, for a discussion of this issue.

10   See Sert, "New York: Architecture and the City" (1955), included in this book.

11   Eric Mumford, "Josep Lluís Sert: The CIAM Heart of the City and the Bogotá Plan. Precursor to Urban Design, 1947-1953," in Maria Cecilia O'Byrne Orozco, ed., *Le Corbusier en Bogotá, 1947-1951* (Bogotá: Ediciones Uniandes, 2010), 2: 240-49.

12   Town Planning Associates, *Plan Piloto de Habana* (Havana, 1958). For a detailed historical discussion of the planning and political context of this plan, see Timothy Hyde, *A Constitutional Modernism: Architecture and Civil Society in the Cuban Republic* (Minneapolis: University of Minnesota Press, 2013), and Eduardo Luis Rodriguez, *The Havana Guide* (New York: Princeton University Press, 2000), vii-xxxvi.

13   Jane Jacobs, then a journalist for *Architectural Forum*, first voiced her ideas about the importance of pedestrian urban street life at Sert's First Harvard Urban Design Conference in 1956. See Jacobs's remarks in "Urban Design," *Progressive Architecture* 37 (August 1956): 102-3.

CHAPTER 1

1   For a more detailed discussion of how Sert and others shifted the postwar discourse of CIAM toward a focus on the political and cultural "heart of the city," see Eric Mumford, *The CIAM Discourse on Urbanism, 1928-60* (Cambridge, MA: MIT Press, 2000), 201-14, and *Defining Urban Design: CIAM Architects and the Formation of a Discipline, 1937-69* (New Haven: Yale University Press, 2009), 80-88.

CHAPTER 2

1   See Alison Smithson, ed., *Team 10 Primer* (Cambridge, MA: MIT Press, 1968); Max Risselada and Dirk van den Heuvel, eds., *Team 10: In Search of a Utopia of the Present, 1953-81* (Rotterdam: NAi, 2006).

CHAPTER 3

1 In the typescript, the sentence originally began with "As a result of this attitude."

CHAPTER 4

1 Joan Ockman, "The War Years in America: New York, Monumentality," in Xavier Costa, ed., *Sert: Architect in New York* (Barcelona: MACBA, 1997), 22-45.

CHAPTER 5

1 Alexander Garvin, *The American City: What Works, What Doesn't* (New York: McGraw-Hill, 2002), 436-37.
2 "Fresh Meadows," in Kenneth T. Jackson, ed., *The Encyclopedia of New York City* (New Haven: Yale University Press, 1995), 441-42.

CHAPTER 6

1 The Team 10 contributions to this event are illustrated in Max Risselada and Dirk van den Heuvel, eds., *Team 10: In Search of a Utopia of the Present, 1953-81* (Rotterdam: NAi, 2006), 50-59, and in the articles in *Rassegna* (Milan) 52, no. 4 (December 1992).
2 On Arne Korsmo, see Christian Norberg-Schulz, *The Functionalist Arne Korsmo* (Oslo: Universitetsforlaget, 1986).

CHAPTER 8

1 José Luis Sert, "The Architect and the City," in H. W. Dunham, ed., *The City in Mid-Century: Prospects for Human Relations in the Urban Environment* (Detroit: Wayne State University Press, 1957). In 1954, Wayne State began building out a new low-rise campus masterplan by Minoru Yamasaki that followed many of the same principles Sert would advocate at Harvard a few years later, and Sert selected Yamasaki as the architect of the highrise William James Hall at Harvard (1963).
2 Richard A. Miller, "Density by Design," *Architectural Forum* 110 (March 1959): 130-35.

CHAPTER 9

1 Sandy Isenstadt, "U.S. Embassy," and Patricia Juncosa, "Fondation Maeght," in Josep M. Rovira, ed., *Sert, 1928-1979* (Barcelona: Miro Foundation, 2007), 235-45, 207-17. Sert later gave a clear account of his ideas about architectural pedagogy at GSD at the Twelfth Congress of the International Union of Architects, held in Madrid in May 1975. The original Spanish text and an English translation, "How to Stimulate Architectural Creativity," is in Jaume Freixa, *Josep Lluís Sert* (Barcelona: Santa and Cole, 2005), 214-23.

CHAPTER 15

1 Many of these projects, of which a number were built, are photographically documented in Roloff Beny, *Iran: Elements of Destiny* (New York: Everest House, 1978), 326-61.
2 Letter from Amir H. Sharifi to Sert, July 15, 1974 (Sert Collection, Frances Loeb Library, Harvard Graduate School of Design, Folder E62). Others invited included Hans Hollein, Arthur Erickson, Moshe Safdie, Jorn Utzon, James Stirling, Georges Candilis, Michel Ecochard, Bruno Zevi, Leonardo Benevolo, Kyonori Kikutake, Fumihiko Maki, Kenzo Tange, Dolf Schnebli, and Hassan Fathy.

TEXT SOURCES

All texts are from Josep Lluís Sert Collection, Frances Loeb Library Special Collections, Harvard Graduate School of Design (JLS) unless noted here.

1 "The Theme of the Congress: The Core" (1951) (CIAM 8—The Festival Congress—July 1951, opening address—J. L. Sert) (gta archives, ETH Zurich: CIAM archives 42-JT-6-36/41).
2 "The Neighborhood Unit: A Human Measure in City Planning" (n.d., circa 1953) (JLS Folder D100).
3 "Urban Design" (1953) (JLS Folder D91).
4 "Architecture and the Visual Arts," *Harvard Foundation for Advanced Study and Research Newsletter* (Dec. 31, 1954), 6-8.
5 "New York: Architecture and the City" (1955) (JLS Folder D30).
6 "CIAM X, Dubrovnik" (1956), opening and closing remarks, pp. 14-19, 38-40 (gta archives, ETH Zurich: CIAM archives).
7 "Harvard: Urban Problem and Opportunity," *Harvard Today* (November 1957): 2-10.
8 "The Human Scale: Key to the Measure of Cities" (1957) (JLS Folder D17).
9 "Architectural Fashions and the People" (1959) (JLS Folder D50).
10 "Boston: A Lively and Human City" (JLS Folder D4; *Boston Globe Sunday Magazine,* March 15, 1964).
11 Eighth Urban Design Conference, Harvard Graduate School of Design, "The Role of Government in the Form and Animation of the Urban Core" (1964).
12 "Open Spaces and Pedestrian Paths in the University," Harvard University Planning Office, *Harvard University, 1960: An Inventory for Planning* (also JLS Folder D13).
13 "Sigfried Giedion in Memoriam" (1968) (JLS Folder D12).
14 "Architecture and the People: There Are Two Histories of Architecture" (1972) (JLS Folder D48).
15 "Industrialization: An Opportunity for the Design of New Communities" (1974) (JLS Folder D72).
16 "Balance in the Human Habitat" (1977) (JLS Folder D52).

INDEX

Numbers in *italics* indicate illustrations.

Aalto, Alvar, 134
Abrams, Charles, xvii
Agra (India), settlement near (sketch; Sert), *126*
Alexandria, Egypt, 136
American Embassy (Baghdad; Sert), 92
Andrews, John, xvii
Antoni Gaudí (Sert and Sweeney book), 42
Apthorp House (Cambridge, MA), *116*
The Architects Collaborative (TAC), 75
architecture, xv, 34, 40, 44-49, 55, 61, 127, 128, 142: changes in, 22, 50, 77, 95; climate's importance in, 92, 95; contemporary, 38, 50; dehumanization in, 87; functionalist, 48, 52; historic styles of, 38; modern, 134-36; revolution in, 44, 92-93; satisfying human needs, 75; structure's importance in, 92, 96; vocabulary of, 50, 95
Ardalan, Nader, 148
Aristotle, 90
Athens Charter of 1933 (CIAM), 58, 59-60
Augur, Tracy, 34
automobiles. *See cars*

Back Bay (Boston), 100-101, 103, 105
Bacon, Edmund N., xv, xvii, 77
Baghdad Civic Center (sketch; Sert), 94
Bakema, Jacob, 58
Balanced Habitat (Sert), xv, xviii, 147
Banares (India), settlement near (sketch; Sert), *126*
Bauer, Catherine, 108
BBPR (Milan), 65
Belgiojoso, Lodovico, 66
Belt Route (Boston), 72
Benjamin Thompson Associates, 102
Biblioteca Luis Ángel Arango (Bogotá; Samper), 66
Billerica (MA), residential sector core for (HGSD students), *81*
Bogotá (Colombia), planning for, xvii
Bogotá Masterplan (Town Planning Associates), 20
Boston, 131-32; core of, 109-10; highway system for, 72; masterplan for, 100, 105-6; park system in, 100; skyline of, 101, 106; waterfront renewal, proposed (Boston Redevelopment Authority), *109*. *See also* Cambridge (MA)
Boston Public Library (McKim, Mead & White), *103*
Boston Redevelopment Authority, 100
Boston University, xiii
Boston University Law and Education Schools tower (Sert, Jackson with Steffian), 101

Bottoni, Piero (Milan), 66
BRA. *See* Boston Redevelopment Authority
Brazilian Motor City (Town Planning Associates), xiv
Brera, Georges (Geneva), 68
Brooklyn Bridge, 50
Building Systems, Inc., 152
Bulfinch, Charles, 100, 101

Calder, Alexander, 42, 45, 122
Cali (Colombia), 3
Cambridge (MA), 70-72; historical development of, 76; masterplan for, 112. *See also Harvard listings*
Cambridge Planning Board, 71
Candela, Felix, 92, 98
Candilis, Georges, 12, 58, 134, 148
Can Our Cities Survive? (Sert), xiii-xv, 145
Carpenter Center for the Visual Arts (Harvard University; Le Corbusier with Sert, Jackson), vii, *105*
cars, 8, 24-25, 72; effect of, on cities' growth, 81; growing use of, 90. *See also* commuting; highways; parking; sprawl
Center for the Study of World Religions (Harvard University; Sert, Jackson & Gourley,), vii, ix
central business districts, 136
Central Europe, housing in, 21
Charles Luckman & Associates, 101
Charles River (Boston), 100, 105, 120
Charter of Habitat (CIAM), 58, 59, 134
Charter of Urban Rights (United Nations), 142
Chermayeff, Serge, xviii
Chicago Land Clearance Commission, 30
Chimbote (Peru), 145; Masterplan (Town Planning Associates), 18; sketch of human-scale elements (Sert), *82*; tapis urbain for, 39
CIAM (Congrès Internationaux d'Architecture Moderne [International Congresses for Modern Architecture]), vii, xiii, 12, 63, 122-24, 145, 148; CIAM 5 (Paris, 1937), 60; CIAM 6 (Bridgwater, England), 60; CIAM 7 (Bergamo, Italy, 1949), 60; CIAM 8 (Hoddesdon, England, 1951), 60; CIAM 9 Aix-en-Provence, France, 1953), 60; division in, 58; force behind, 60; future of, 61-68; grid, 60, 61, 63; groups in, personalities of, 95; growth of, 63, 64; humanistic approach of, 2; new structure for, 58; pioneering work of, 2; prewar, xvi; Sert's last public comments to, 58-68
CIAM 8: The Heart of the City (Tyrwhitt, Sert, and Rogers), xiii-xv, *3, 60*
CIAM GATCPAC (Barcelona; Grup d'Arquitectes Catalans Per Una Arquitectura Contemporánea), 13

CIRPAC, 61, 63
cities, 40, 88, 132, 144-45: advantages of, 2-5; attitude toward, 38; changes in, xvii, 30, 34, 38, 52, 81, 84; chaos in, 14; conditions in, poor, 134, 142, 144-45; core of, 2-9; criticisms of, 34; decentralization of, 2; destruction of, 5; development of, 49; expressing a culture, 88-90; human needs in, overlooked, 14, 15; large populations in, 28; migration to, 144-45; as mother of the arts, 90; neighborhood units in relation to, 27; organic nature of, 28; overextension of, 5, 12, 27; scale of, 14-15, 28; shapelessness of, 128; traffic in, 8. See also city planning
Citizens' Advisory Committee (Cambridge, MA), 71
Citizens Housing Council (New York), 145
city code revision, 30-31
City Hall Plaza (Boston), 100
city planning, xv, 2, 9, 14, 22, 28, 40, 142; accounting for the human condition, 82-83, 85-87; advances in, 15-16; commissions for, 31; flexibility in, 12; goal of, 46; three-dimensional approach to, 34, 40
civic culture, 40
civic design: joint effort of, 38; moving to the suburbs, 2
civic space, 10
climate, 26, 92, 95
Collins, Mayor John (Boston), 100
communication: city cores and, 6; new systems of, 22
communities, 9, 14, 138; commercial buildings in, 19-20; compact, 138-41; experimental, 142; flexible formulas for, 22; prototypes, 148; qualitative issues with, 149; services for, 16-20, 21, 23
community center (club), 19
community units, 28
commuting, 29-30
congestion, 70-71, 148
Conklin & Rossant (New York; Butterfield House apartments; Reston, VA), 89
cores, 2-9, 84, 109-10
Corso Francia apartments (Turin; BBPR), 65
cuadras (square blocks), viii, 14
Cuba, xiii, xv, xvii, 70, 157
culture, city-made, 14
Cushing, Cardinal Richard James, 104
Cuzco (Peru), 5

decentralization, 2, 5, 55, 81
density, 20, 24-26, 55, 148
Doebele, William, 148

Doshi, Balkrishna, 134, 148
double-hung sash, human scale of, 48, 87
Drew, Jane, xviii

Ecole des Beaux-Arts (Besançon, France; model; Sert), *131*
Eisenhower, President Dwight D., 90
England, garden cities in, 21
environment, complete, building of, 38
environmental studies, schools of, 142
Esguerra, Sáenz, Urdaneta, Samper (Bogotá), 66
ETH Zurich, 124

Faneuil Hall Marketplace (Boston; Benjamin Thompson Associates), *102*
Fondation Maeght (France; Sert), 92
form, function and, 44-45, 75, 95
Fresh Meadows (Queens, NY; Voorhees, Walker, Foley & Smith), 48, 53, *54*
Frioul Islands, France, 127, 130
Fry, Maxwell, xviii, 12
Fuller, R. Buckminster, 134
Functional City, xv
functionalism, 40, 49, 52

garden cities, 24
Gaudí, Antoni, 42
Giedion, Sigfried, 58, 62 66, 122-24; *Space, Time and Architecture* (Giedion), *122*; *Architecture and the Phenomenon of Transition* (Giedion), 122; *Eternal Present, The* (Giedion), 122Giedion-Welcker, Carola, 124
Government Center chapel (Boston; model; Sert), *104*
Goyette, Harold, 70, 113
Grand Central Concourse (New York), 50
greenbelts, 21, 28, 119
green spaces, 74
Gropius, Walter, xv, 61, 68, 75, 122
Group X, see Team 10
Guernica (Picasso), 42
Guévrékian, Gabriel, 68
Gulick, Luther, 90

habitat: CIAM definitions of, 59; total concept of, 60
Habitat Bill of Rights (United Nations), 144, 145, 148-50
Habitat II conference (United Nations, Vancouver 1976), xviii
Harrison, Ballard & Allen (New York), 48, 52-53
Harvard Graduate Center (Gropius and TAC), 75

Harvard Square, 71, 72
Harvard University, xiii; development of, 72; expansion of, 70, 74-78; Harvard Yard, *73*, 115; Office of the Planning Coordinator, 70, 71-72; Old Yard, 112; open spaces at, 74, 112, 115-20; parking at, 72; pedestrian movement at, 112; pedestrian pathway system (Sert and Harvard University Planning Office), *113*; urban campus of, 70-71
Harvard University Center for the Study of World Religions (Cambridge, MA; Sert, Jackson & Gourley), 93
Harvard University Graduate School of Design, viii, xiii, xv, 42-46
Harvard University Planning Office, 113
Harvard University Science Center (Sert, Jackson), vii-viii, *x*, xi, 70, *118*
Harvard University, 1960: An Inventory for Planning, 112, 113
Harvard Urban Design conferences, 80, 108-10
Harvard Urban Design Program, 70
Havana, presidential palace in, 70
Havana Master Plan (Sert and Wiener), xvii, 70
highways, 80, 84, 138
Hoddesdon Congress (CIAM 8, 1951), 60
Holden Chapel (Harvard Yard), *73*
Holmes, Oliver Wendell, 101
Holyoke Center (Harvard University; Sert, Jackson & Gourley), vii, xi, 70, *114*, *116*
Hong Kong, 136
housing: density of, 141; housing programs, 21-22; housing projects, 12, 14; light wall units for, 53; qualitative issues with, 149
Howe, George, 34
Hudnut, Dean Joseph, xv
human condition, city planning and, 82-83, 85-86
human habitat, code of, 147, 153
human needs, 61: architecture satisfying, 75; disregard for, 14, 15
human rights, 153
Human Settlements, xviii

Ibler, Drago (Zagreb, Croatia), 58, 63, 67, 68
India, sketches from (Sert), *127*
industrialization, 134, 138
international style, 92, 93
interstate system, federal, 80-81
Iranian International Congress of Architects, 134, 145-47
Iranian Ministry of Housing and Urban Development, 148
Isfahan (Iran), drawings from (Sert), *135*

Jacobs, Jane, xvii
Jeanneret, Pierre, xviii
Johansen, John, 152
John Hancock Insurance Company tower (Boston; I. M. Pei & Partners), *101*
Johnson, President Lyndon B., 108
Justement, Louis (Washington, DC), 34

Kahn, Louis, xv
Kasbah Fadala (Tunisia), *129*
Kennedy, President John F., 153
Kittelsen, Grete Prytz (Oslo), 62
Kondracki, Georges, 148
Korn, Arthur, 12
Korsmo, Arne (Oslo), 61, 62

La Candelaria (Old City, Bogotá), aerial view, *xiv*, 15
land: abuse of, 148; consolidation of, in cities, 30–31; taxation and, 128; value of, 25, 26, 38; waste of, 70–71
landscape architecture, xv, 46, 142
land-use planning, 6
layer-cake buildings (New York City), 50, 87
Le Corbusier, xviii, 12, 35, 58, 61, 105, 128; approach of, to urban planning, 34; criticism of, 136; CIAM grid system of, 60; impact of, vii, 97, 148; Sert's connection with, vii, 70; Sert's proposals differing from, xvi–xvii
Léger, Fernand, 122
Lemco, Blanche, 66
Lever House (New York; Skidmore, Owings & Merrill), 48, 51, 52
Lima, Peru, 145
Lincoln Building (New York), 50
Lipchitz, Jacques, 122
Llewelyn-Davies, Richard, 134
Logue, Edward, 100, 110, 152
Los Angeles, 90
Louisburg Square (Boston), descriptive historical plaque from, *103*

MacIver, Robert M., 14n
Maki, Fumihiko (Tokyo), xvii, xviii
Manhattan House (New York; SOM), 52
MARS group (Britain), 2, 6, 9
MARS Plan of London (1938-41), 12
Martin, Sir Leslie, 66
Martin Luther King, Jr., public school (Cambridge, MA; Sert, Jackson; demolished), 150
Massachusetts State House (Boston; Charles Bulfinch and others), *101*

mass transportation, 25
master planning, rejection of, xvii
master of urban design program, xvii
McGregor Conference center (Detroit; Minoru Yamasaki), 95
McHarg, Ian, 134
McKim, Mead & White, 103
measure, sense of, 14–15
Medellín (Colombia), master plan for, 7
"Mercury Fountain" (Calder), 42
Meyer, Hannes, 58
Mies van der Rohe, Ludwig, vii, 66
Miró, Joan, 42
Miró Studio (Sert), 42, *43*
mixed-income housing, xiii
mixed-use development (Exposition Park, Lima; Town Planning Associates), 35
mixed-use housing, 140, 144
modernism, xvii, 92, 93
Mumford, Lewis, 34, 48

neighborhoods: community services of, 16–19; personality of, 12; planning of, 16–19
neighborhood units, vii, 12, 16-32; diagrammatic plan for (Sert), *17*; theoretical pattern of, *17*
Nervi, Pier Luigi, 92, 96
Neumann, Arieh (Israel), 66
"New Communities" (sketch; Sert), *139*
New Urbanism, xvi, 48
New York City, 53, 55, 56, 90; architectural courage of, 49–50; layer-cake buildings in, 50; new look for, 48, 55; zoning and building codes in, 48, 52–53
New York State Urban Development Corporation, xvii–xviii, 140, 145, 152–53
Nivola, Constantino, viii, xi
Nixon (President Richard M.) administration, 153

Olmsted, Frederick Law, 100, 112
Ortega y Gasset, José, 9–10; The *Revolt of the Masses* (Ortega y Gasset), 9–10
Ozenfant, Amedée, 122

Pahlavi, Farah, 134
palaces, plan comparisons of (Town Planning Associates), 97
Palazzetto dello Sport (Rome; Nervi), *96*
Pan-American Congress of Architects, 64
Paris: Harvard GSD student scale analysis drawing of , *36*; plan of (Town Planning Associates), 37
Paris City University, Brazilian pavilion at (Le Corbusier), 97

parking, 8, 106: accompanying new construction, 52, 72; peripheral, 55, 87, 138
Parris, Alexander, 102
patio houses, 145
Peabody Terrace Married Student Housing (Harvard University; Sert, Jackson), vii, xv, 70, *120*, 144, 145, *146*, 150-52
pedestrian cities, xv-xvii
pedestrian precinct: guidelines for (Sert), *147*; mixed-use, land-use recommendations for, 145
pedestrians, 131; central areas for, xvi; islands for, 8; measuring community by, 138; movement of, human scale for; protection of, 26
Pei, I. M., xvii, 101, 134
Perkins, George Holmes, 34
Perry, Clarence, 12
Persepolis Congress (Iran), 144, 145-47
Peru, low-cost housing in, 18
Picasso, Pablo, 42, 97
planning: extremist attitudes in, 148; necessity of, 71
Plan Piloto de la Habana (Sert), 97
Plan for the Rezoning of the City of New York (Harrison, Ballard & Allen), 48, 52-53
play field space, 117
pollution, 134-36
population, density of, 26-27, 138
prefabrication, 53
presidential palace project (Havana; Town Planning Associates, with Candela), *98*
Prudential Center (Boston; Charles Luckman & Associates), *101*
Pruitt-Igoe complex (St. Louis; Hellmuth, Yamasaki & Leinweber), xvi
public square, 6, 10
public transportation, 138
Pusey, Nathan, 108

quadrangles, in educational settings, 74
Quincy House (Harvard University; Shepley Bulfinch Richardson & Abbott), *117*
Quincy Market (Boston; Parris), *102*

Radburn (NJ), plan for, 12
Radcliffe Yard (Cambridge, MA), 115
Rapson, Ralph, 134
recentralization, 5, 84
Redevelopment Act (1956), 80
Regional Plan of New York and Environs (1929), 12
regional planning, xv, 142
residential sectors, design of, challenges in, 132

resorts, 136
Reston (VA), 89
Rio de Janeiro (Brazil), 136, 145
Riverview apartment complex (Yonkers, NY; Sert, Jackson), *151*
Rockefeller Center, 52
Rogers, Ernesto, xvi, 58, 65, 66
Ronchamp (chapel of Notre Dame du Haut; Le Corbusier), 97
Roosevelt (President Franklin D.) administration, 21
Roosevelt Island (New York; Sert, Jackson), xiii, xv, xviii, *140*, 144
Roth, Alfred (Zurich), 58, 63
row housing, 25
Rowe, Colin, 97
Rudofsky, Bernard, 127, 131

Saarinen, Eliel, 34
Safdie, Moshe, 148
Samper, Germán (Bogotá), 66
Samuely, Felix, 12
San Francisco, 131-32, 136
Sasaki, Dawson, DeMay, 101
Sasaki, Hideo, xvii
SBRA (Shepley Bulfinch Richardson & Abbott), 117
scale, 14-15, 48, 85; vertical and horizontal, 87; violation of, 136
Schuette, Wilhelm (Vienna), 68
Schulz, Paul, xiv
sector spaces, 115
segregation and the neighborhood unit, 28
Sekler, Eduard, xvii
semirural life, planning for, 27
Sert, Josep Lluís, xiv, *13*, 39, *45*, *49*, 87, *104*, *123*, 148; advocating pedestrian cities, xv-xvi; campus planning of, for Harvard, 70; creating Harvard University Office of the Planning Coordinator, 70; criticism of, xvii; developing a new profession, xv; founding Harvard University Planning Office, 113; historical importance of, xvi; involved in the art world, 42; association of, with Le Corbusier, vii; larger buildings of, criticism of, viii-xi; last public comments to CIAM, 58-68; later works of, xviii; launching first master of urban design program, xvii; legacy of, xiii; role of, in CIAM, 58; social interaction in projects of, vii; urban references in U.S. projects, vii-viii; using urban design to link other design elements, xv
Sert, Jackson & Associates, 101, 105, 118, 120, 130, 131, 140, 151

164 INDEX

Sert, Jackson & Gourley, 116
Sert House (Cambridge, MA), *85*
shelter spaces (cells), human scale for, 85-87
Shiraz (Iran), drawings from (Sert), *135*
Skidmore, Owings & Merrill, 48
Smith Campus Center (Harvard University Holyoke Center), xi
Smithson, Alison, 58
Smithson, Peter, 58, 68
social services: in a community, 19, 20; payment for, 23
solar cycle, 14
Soltan, Jerzy, xvii, 66
Samonà, Giuseppe (Italy), 66
sprawl, 80-81, 83, 131, 148
Steffian, Edwin T. (Boston), 101
suburbanism, 2, 34
suburbs, 108; commuting and, 30; growth of, 53, 80; industry moving to, 15; overextension of, 5
superfluous, human need for, 95-96
Sweeney, James Johnson, 42
Syrkus, Helena (Warsaw), 61, 66
Syrkus, Szymon (Warsaw), 66

Tange, Kenzo (Japan), 134
tapis urbain (urban fabric), 39
Team 10, xvi, xvii, xviii, 12, 58, 61, 63
Temple University (Philadelphia), 70, 77
Tennessee Valley Authority, 144
Terrace Plaza Hotel (Cincinnati, OH; Skidmore, Owings & Merrill), 42
Thailand, sketches from (Sert), *127*
Thompson, Benjamin (Boston), 102
Times Square (New York City), 55
Town Planning Associates, xiv, 3, 70, 97, 98; brochure for, *13*; New York office, *49*
Tracoba Systems, 152
travel, energy use in, 84
Tsoi, Edward (Boston), 148
Tyrwhitt, Jaqueline, xvi, xvii, 58, 63, 67, 83, 122, 148

UDC. *See* New York State Urban Development Corporation
Ungers, O. M. (Berlin), 134
Unite d'Habitation (Marseilles; Le Corbusier), 136
Unité model, xvii
United Nations, xiii, xviii, 144, 145, 148-50; headquarters of (New York), 48, 52
United States: cities in, destruction of, xvi; northeast of, 80; federal housing projects in, 21; interstate system in, xvi; National Patent Office, 122
universities, setting an example for pedestrian green spaces in cities, 112
urban design, vii-viii, 34, 108, 110; architecture extending into, 95; daily experience and, 80; growth of, 86; as professional field, xvi
urban fragment, viii
urbanism, 2, 34, 60; prewar, xvi; Sert's importance to, xvi
urban perception, speeds of (drawing; Sert), *137*
urban planning. *See* city planning
urban regions, 80-81, 83
urban renewal, xvi, xvii
urban sectors, breaking regions into, 83-84
U.S. Steel, 70
utility spaces, 117-19

Van der Broek, J. H. (Rotterdam), 66
Van Eesteren, Cornelis (Amsterdam), 61, 66
Van Eyck, Aldo, 58
Van Ginkel, Blanche Lemco, 66
van Tijen, Willem (Rotterdam), 58
Venezuela, 70
vernacular, influence of, on architecture, 127-28
visual arts, 42-44
Von Eckardt, Wolf, 110
Von Moltke, Willo, xvii, 70, 77
Voorhees, Walker, Smith & Smith (New York), 48
Voorhees Walker, Foley & Smith (New York), 48, 54

Wagner, Mayor Robert F. (New York), 48
Walker, Ralph, 48
Wallace, McHarg, Roberts & Todd, 134
Washington, DC: Harvard GSD student scale analysis drawing of, *36*; planning of, 34
Weaver, Robert C., xvii, 108, 110
Weiner, Irving (Harvard GSD student), 36
Weissmann, Ernest, 12
Wiener, Paul Lester, xiv, xvii, 12, 13, 39, 49, 70
Woefflin, Heinrich, 124
Wooden Tower (Zagreb; Ibler), 67
Woods, Shadrach, xvii, 12

Yamasaki, Minoru (Detroit), 92, 95, 158n1 (chap. 8)
Yonkers (NY), xiii, xv, xviii, 144

zoning, 30-31, 48
Zurich Polytechnic Institute (ETH Zurich), 124

ILLUSTRATION CREDITS

The photographers and the sources of visual material other than the owners indicated in the captions are as follows. Every effort has been made to supply complete and correct credits; if there are errors or omissions, please contact Yale University Press so that corrections can be made in any subsequent edition. Numbers refer to page numbers in this book.

Courtesy Center for Creative Photography, University of Arizona ©1991 Hans Namuth Estate: 49

Courtesy Croatian Society of Architects, courtesy of Ivan Rupnik: 67

Ekistics 18, no. 105 (August 1964): 109 (page 9)

Gottscho-Schleisner Collection, Library of Congress: 7

gta archives, ETH Zurich, CIAM archives: 59

Harvard Today, November 1957: 76 (page 8), 77 (page 9)

Harvard University Graduate School of Design, *Comparative Housing Study* (1958), page 163: 81

Historic American Buildings Survey (HABS), Arthur C. Haskell, Photographer. March, 1934. view from west; HABS MASS, 9-CAMB, 3c-2, Library of Congress: 73

Eric Mumford: xi (2014), 15 (2010), 51 (2003), 65 (2006), 66 (2010), 71 (2010), 75 (2010), 89 (2006), 93 (2004), 95 (2010), 101 top (2013), 102 (2012); 103 top (2004), 105 (2012), 114 (2004), 116 bottom (2004), 117 (2004), 118 (2012), 120 (2004), 124 (2009)

© Steve Rosenthal: 151

Josep Lluís Sert Collection, Frances Loeb Library, Harvard Graduate School of Design: ix, x, xiii, xiv, 4, 5, 17 top, 18, 20, 35–37, 39, 43 (Català-Roca), 45, 82, 83, 85, 87, 94, 97, 98, 104, 113, 116 top, 120, 126, 127, 129–31, 135, 137, 139, 140, 145, 146 (Lawrence Lowry), 147

Mary Ann Sullivan: 96

Thomas Airviews, New York Life Archives: 54

Town Planning Review, June 1935, page 251: 17 bottom

Universitetsforlaget, Oslo: 62

Used with permission of W. Colston Leigh, Inc.: 13

Wikipedia Commons: 101 bottom